EXPANDING THE
Primary Writer's Workshop

50 Mini-Lessons to Improve Writing

Written by Carol Kieczykowski

Fearon Teacher Aids
A Division of Frank Schaffer Publications, Inc.

To my husband, Ed, for his constant
support and encouragement.

To Mary Jo, for being the best friend anyone could
ever have and for being able to turn ideas into reality.

To Rene, for being my #1 photographer and
for assisting with the layout of many of the
forms in this guide.

To Rita, for always connecting me with children's
books I couldn't resist.

To visionary teachers like Pam H., Jackie, Kerry,
Katie, Gretchen, Pam F., and Dorothy, who are
willing to try out some of my ideas and share samples
of their students' work.

Editors: Lisa Trumbauer, Kristin Eclov, Christine Hood

Cover Illustration: William Sheifer

Book Design and Graphics: Rose Sheifer

Book Illustration: Joyce John

© Fearon Teacher Aids
A Division of Frank Schaffer Publications, Inc.
23740 Hawthorne Boulevard
Torrance, CA 90505-5927

Fearon Teacher Aids products were formerly manufactured and distributed by American
Teaching Aids, Inc., a subsidiary of Silver Burdett Ginn, and are now manufactured and
distributed by Frank Schaffer Publications, Inc. FEARON, FEARON TEACHER AIDS, and the
FEARON balloon logo are marks used under license from Simon & Schuster, Inc.

Contents

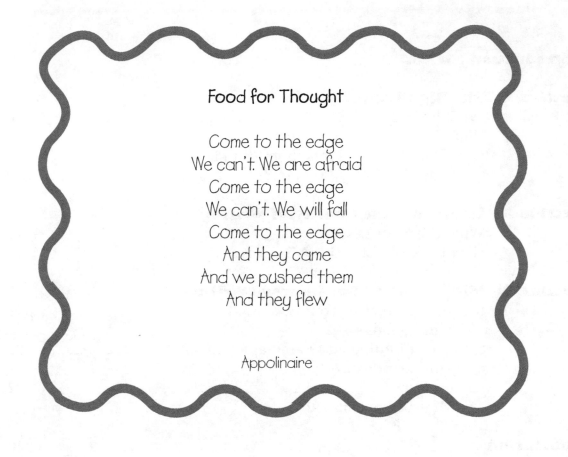

Food for Thought

Come to the edge
We can't. We are afraid
Come to the edge
We can't. We will fall
Come to the edge
And they came
And we pushed them
And they flew

Appolinaire

Introduction

I received the poem on the previous page many years ago while taking a class on process writing. It made me realize, as I hope you will, what a carefully orchestrated task it is to create real writers, especially at the primary level. In a nutshell, and not to sound too intimidating—*we are it!* We, as teachers, are the first building blocks for these young authors-to-be. And *every* child can be an author. We must teach them the elements of wonderful writing, while at the same time, help them develop a love for the *process* of writing. We must be accepting and validating at each step along the way, but we must never accept second best. Each writer must be brought along at the appropriate speed, but not at the expense of quality. We must set up the necessary scaffolding so that when children come to the edge, as described in the poem, they will *not* be afraid. They will *not* fall. We must push with our knowledge and carefully selected modeling so that one day, they *will* fly!

Since the publication of my last teacher resource book, *Primary Writer's Workshop* (Fearon Teacher Aids, 1996), I have continued to give inservices and teach university-level courses for teachers on teaching writing to young children. The feedback I have received from both sources is the same—Teachers want and need more information on process writing at the primary level. *Primary Writer's Workshop* is helpful for getting started and providing primary teachers with the scaffolding necessary to teach process writing. But when it comes to taking the next step, to creating real writers, teachers need a guide to assist them in planning and delivering mini-lessons. This latest guide is an attempt to fill that request.

As I look back over the years as a primary writing teacher, I don't think that I was creating real writers until I became more skilled in developing mini-lessons and in following my students' lead. Some teachers are so busy writing with their students that they never take time to deliver meaningful mini-lessons. The only way to improve the quality of writing in any classroom is through frequent and specific writing instruction. In a workshop setting, this instruction includes modeling and carefully designed lessons that are often tied back to real literature. Once students become aware that very specific features characterize all "good writing," they are then able to critically analyze and improve their *own* writing. Quality writing really takes off when teachers can plan mini-lessons around these traits. Mini-lessons are truly the heart of a writer's workshop.

It is my hope that this guide will provide specific information on how to plan and deliver powerful mini-lessons, and that it will inspire you to teach the elements of wonderful writing. Remember—wonderful writers are not born, but they can be molded and encouraged.

Good Luck!

Carol Kieczykowski

What Is Process Writing?

The biggest gift that process-writing teachers give to their students is *TIME*. Create an environment that allows for writing to be revisited over and over again in an attempt to improve such things as wording, fluency, and understanding. In process-writing classrooms, there is no race to the publishing finish line. Revision is not done just because it is one of the steps of the writing process. Rather, this reshaping or polishing of one's work is carefully modeled through mini-lessons and valued as fundamental to good writing.

Process writing cannot be done by simply posting the steps on the wall in a classroom or by simply giving students opportunities to write thoughout the day. You must concretely model each of the steps of the writing process and provide time for writing to take place in a workshop setting. For first graders, consider explaining the steps of the process with "I can" statements such as the following:

The Writing Process

1. I can think. (prewriting)
   Show children how to use a mind map or story structure to organize their thinking.
2. I can write. (drafting)
   Show children how to write a first draft based on a mind map or story structure.
3. I can share. (revising and editing)
   Model a peer conference and show how, through questioning and commenting, one might add, take away, or rearrange writing.

Be sure to have examples of how children's work looks at each of these stages. You may wish to post a chart that outlines these steps and displays rebus pictures as reminders. (See example on page 8. For a more comprehensive look at the presentation of this material, refer to *Primary Writer's Workshop*.)

Tip: Go slowly! Students need time to process these new ideas. Remember—model, model, model! In time, students will begin to understand that good writers go through very specific steps when creating with words.

 © Fearon Teacher Aids FE11021

⭐ What Is Writer's Workshop?

Donald Graves, Lucy Calkins, and Nancie Atwell gave birth to writer's workshop during the early 1980s. Their approach to writing has now become a fundamental part of most language arts curriculums. They have structured their workshop around three main components, each having equal importance in creating real writers:

> 1. Mini-Lessons
> 2. Writing and Conferencing
> 3. Group Sharing

Page 9 contains a description of these components and the suggested time frame for each. If you feel you cannot block out one full hour, four times a week, for the writer's workshop as suggested, you may need to be creative with the scheduling of the three components. You can move mini-lessons and sharing time to other slots during the day, provided you do not skip any component.

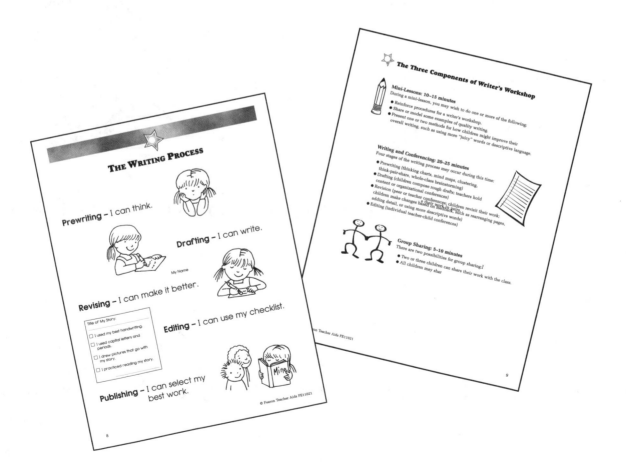

THE WRITING PROCESS

Prewriting – I can think.

Drafting – I can write.

My Name

Revising – I can make it better.

Title of My Story:
☐ I used my best handwriting.
☐ I used capital letters and periods.
☐ I drew pictures that go with my story.
☐ I practiced reading my story.

Editing – I can use my checklist.

Publishing – I can select my best work.

Mine

8

© Fearon Teacher Aids FE11021

⭐ **The Three Components of Writer's Workshop**

Mini-Lessons: 10–15 minutes
During a mini-lesson, you may wish to do one or more of the following:
● Reinforce procedures for a writer's workshop.
● Share or model some examples of quality writing.
● Present one or two methods for how children might improve their overall writing, such as using more "juicy" words or descriptive language.

Writing and Conferencing: 20–25 minutes
Four stages of the writing process may occur during this time:
● Prewriting (thinking charts, mind maps, clustering, think-pair-share, whole-class brainstorming)
● Drafting (children compose rough drafts; teachers hold content or organizational conferences)
● Revision (peer or teacher conferences; children revisit their work; children make changes based on those conferences, such as rearranging pages, adding detail, or using more descriptive words)
● Editing (individual teacher-child conferences)

Group Sharing: 5–10 minutes
There are two possibilities for group sharing:
● Two or three children can share their work with the class.
● All children may share.

9

© Fearon Teacher Aids FE11021

THE WRITING PROCESS

Prewriting – I can think.

Drafting – I can write.

Revising – I can make it better.

Title of My Story:

_____

☐ I used my best handwriting.

☐ I used capital letters and periods.

☐ I drew pictures that go with my story.

☐ I practiced reading my story.

My Name: _____

Editing – I can use my checklist.

Publishing – I can select my best work.

reproducible

The Three Components of Writer's Workshop

Mini-Lessons: 10–15 minutes

During a mini-lesson, you may wish to do one or more of the following:

- Reinforce procedures for a writer's workshop.
- Share or model some examples of quality writing.
- Present one or two methods for how children might improve their overall writing, such as using more "juicy" words or descriptive language.

Writing and Conferencing: 20–25 minutes

Four stages of the writing process may occur during this time:

- Prewriting (thinking charts, mind maps, clustering, think-pair-share, whole-class brainstorming)
- Drafting (children compose rough drafts; teachers hold content or organizational conferences)
- Revision (peer or teacher conferences; children revisit their work; children make changes based on feedback, such as rearranging pages, adding detail, or using more descriptive words)
- Editing (individual teacher-child conferences)

Group Sharing: 5–10 minutes

There are two possibilities for group sharing:

- Two or three children can share their work with the class.
- All children may share their work in pairs.

How Does Writer's Workshop Fit in a Balanced Literacy Program?

A balanced literacy program gives equal importance to the reading and writing components. Provide opportunities throughout the day to foster learning in both reading and writing.

Gay Su Pinnell, in her book *Guided Reading*, provides teachers with a framework to use when developing multiple reading and writing opportunities for students. With regard to writing experiences, she lists four specific types:

1. Shared Writing
2. Interactive Writing
3. Guided Writing
4. Independent Writing

Each type of writing requires a different level of support from the teacher and respects the level of control or independence of the children.

This scaffolding technique is easily understood when the terms *to, with,* and *by themselves* are applied. Throughout the day, teachers must provide opportunities to write *to* their students, to write *with* their students, and to have students write *by themselves*.

Writing to Students

Writing *to* students would include activities such as morning messages, daily news, and language experience stories. With this type of writing, you act as a scribe, modeling proficient writing. See the sample below.

10-23

Good morning children!
We are going to do a
fun art project today.
I think you will enjoy
it.

Writing with Students

Writing *with* students occurs when you and your students share the role of scribe. This is done during *interactive* and *guided writing*. The emphasis here is on assisting students to construct words and begin using the conventions of print. An example of interactive writing can be found below.

Students Writing by Themselves

During writer's workshop, students are invited to write *by themselves*, with little or no support. They independently write using their sound/symbol knowledge, and they often assist each other with the spelling of unknown words.

Since writer's workshop falls into the "independent" category, it is critical that primary teachers target all of these types of writing. Students without modeling and teacher support will never get to this independent stage of composition.

IMPROVING THE QUALITY OF WRITING

One of the most challenging tasks process-writing teachers face is how to improve the quality of their students' writing. To many children, writing is about *quantity* rather than *quality*. They have mistakenly received the message that the best writers are the ones with the most books published. *Product* has been emphasized at the expense of *process*. Editing has become more important than reflection and revision. Only through process writing can teachers hope to create real writers. Effective teaching of process writing takes time, planning, and the knowledge that certain elements are characteristic to good writing. Teachers must learn how to develop and deliver mini-lessons around these elements if they hope to elevate the writing level of their students. Mini-lessons are the key.

What Is a Mini-Lesson?

The term *mini-lesson* describes that part of the writer's workshop in which specific lessons are planned to improve students' writing or to explain the procedures of the workshop itself. These lessons, designed to last about 10–15 minutes, introduce the writer's workshop. Nancie Atwell describes the mini-lesson as "a forum for students to figure out collectively what they know, to think and produce knowledge together, and to lay claim to it as a community of writers."

The most effective mini-lessons for primary writers are those that are *interactive*. Students should be collectively exposed to an element of wonderful writing, and then immediately be given the opportunity to interact with it in a meaningful and engaging way. This collaboration often requires that a mini-lesson exceed the 10–15 minutes suggested in the schedule. It may even run as long as 20–30 minutes. (Students will stay with you because they will be actively involved.)

Mini-lessons for beginning writers should not be rushed. Become an expert at "kid watching." Give your writers what they need, when they need it, with the necessary time to do it well. This may even mean scheduling mini-lessons at other opportune times throughout the day. Be creative and flexible with your mini-lesson schedule. Remember that the mini-lesson is the most powerful tool in improving children's writing. It allows you to deliver quality writing instruction to *all* your students at the same time.

Interactive mini-lessons usually involve the use of real literature children know, overhead transparencies of student work, colorful marking pens, highlighters, self-stick notes, pocket-chart activities, and child-generated lists on chart paper. The modeling, sharing, and generating are done by teachers and students together as a "community of learners."

How to Create Effective Mini-Lessons

1. Let Students Lead You

Mini-lessons are more interesting and powerful when they are taught from children's own writing. Student conferences are an excellent source of topics for future mini-lessons, for conferences let you examine student work individually. For example, when you have conferenced with several students and notice that their stories all lack powerful leads, you could then plan a mini-lesson on beginning sentences that grab the reader.

The best mini-lessons are those in which students are up front at the overhead, modeling for the class. The selection of student writing models can also be done during conference time. Look for students who are proficiently using a particular writing element. Students' work can then be used in a mini-lesson to reinforce this writing feature. Students' writing can be placed on transparencies for the whole class to view during the mini-lesson. What a boost for self-esteem!

On the flip side, choose a student whose writing can be improved in a certain area. Invite that child to the overhead, and, through questioning, proceed with a mini-lesson on sentence stretching or adding details. The student will be equally delighted with the attention received and the ultimate quality of the revised piece.

2. Teach from and Model with Children's Literature

Primary teachers often use *shared reading* and *read-aloud time* as another source of topics for mini-lessons. Because of the reciprocal nature of the reading and writing processes, this can be easily accomplished. While sharing a children's book, students are invited to view it as writers, identifying the features used by the author to engage the reader. The use of children's literature in writing mini-lessons is powerful and effective. Once young writers begin to see that words and stories are put together in very specific ways, they can then begin to improve the quality of their own writing.

3. Develop the Understanding That Good Writing Is Characterized by Specific Features

Many teachers also try to plan mini-lessons around the following elements that are characteristic of good writing:

> Content/Message
> Layout/Flow
> Personality/Style
> Interesting/Precise Words
> Sentence Building and Paragraph Organizing
> Overall Presentation

Only when the art of writing is broken down into specific features and when those features are carefully developed during mini-lessons can writing improve. Enlarge the chart on page 17 that lists and explains these elements of good writing in more detail. These elements should be clearly posted. First-, second-, and third-grade teachers might also include student examples next to each trait. Remember—students learn best from each other. (In Section 3, you will find specific mini-lessons that develop three of these elements.)

4. Provide Meaningful Conferences

Three types of conferences can take place during the Writing and Conferences portions of the Writer's Workshop.

a. Content Conference

The *content* of a student's writing is the focus for this conference. Offer words of praise and encouragement. However, if the writing is to improve, this praise must be very specific and related to the elements of good writing. Listed on pages 18 and 19, in card format, are examples of praise statements that are specific to each element. You may wish to make tagboard copies of these cards. Cut them apart and place them on a ring so they are readily accessible during conference time.

Tip! Remember—content conferencing can also be a source of topics for future mini-lessons. Only through examination of student work can you plan mini-lessons that will move the writing. Goal-setting is also addressed at this time. For example, when a teacher has conferenced with a student and notices that the word *said* is used much too frequently, you can suggest that "using words other than *said*" become a goal for that student.

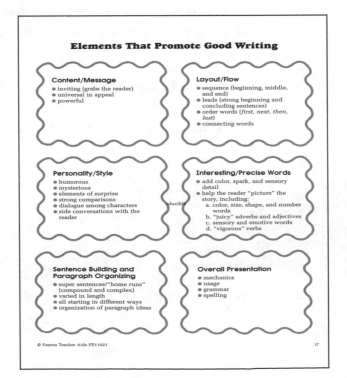

Elements That Promote Good Writing

Content/Message
- inviting (grabs the reader)
- universal in appeal
- powerful

Layout/Flow
- sequence (beginning, middle, and end)
- leads (strong beginning and concluding sentences)
- order words (*first, next, then, last*)
- connecting words

Personality/Style
- humorous
- mysterious
- elements of surprise
- strong comparisons
- dialogue among characters
- side conversations with the reader

Interesting/Precise Words
- add color, spark, and sensory detail
- help the reader "picture" the story, including:
  a. color, size, shape, and number words
  b. "juicy" adverbs and adjectives
  c. sensory and emotive words
  d. "vigorous" verbs

Sentence Building and Paragraph Organizing
- super sentences/"home runs" (compound and complex)
- varied in length
- all starting in different ways
- organization of paragraph ideas

Overall Presentation
- mechanics
- usage
- grammar
- spelling

© Fearon Teacher Aids FE11021   17

b. Peer Conference

This type of meeting takes place between two students. One student is the reader, while the other is the listener. The listener must compliment the writer. The praise should be specific and related to the elements of good writing. For example, "I really like the way you described the waves as gigantic. It helped me picture the storm on the beach." (Writing Element: Interesting/Precise Words)

Conferences become focused when students are looking for a targeted element of good writing. With that in mind, encourage students to use check-off sheets. These sheets, found on pages 20–30, help make conferences more meaningful and manageable for young students. Choose the sheets that relate to a current mini-lesson. Demonstrate how to use the sheets, then make them available in your peer conference corners. You might also ask that the sheets be clipped to the child's writing.

Again, modeling is the secret to establishing effective peer conferences. Be sure students understand the following steps:

- Read and listen
- Compliment (specific to writing elements)
- Question and offer suggestions
- Check off items on conference sheets
- Find and highlight items on conference sheets

Tip! Don't hold students accountable for checking off all the elements at once. Build as you go, adding one thing at a time. If you work on everything at once, students will become overwhelmed and get lost in a sea of check-off sheets. In this instance, less is more!

★Content Conference Chart
(Writing Element—Interesting Words)

Title of my story: _____

_____

My friend and I will check for interesting words.

☐ 1. I used color words, like: ☐ 2. I used number words, like:

_____   _____

_____   _____

_____   _____

My Name: _____

My Friend's Name: _____

*Use highlighters to mark any color or number words in your work!

© Fearon Teacher Aids FE11021   reproducible   21

★Content Conference Chart
(Writing Element—Interesting Words)

Title of my story: _____

_____

My friend and I will check for interesting words.

☐ 1. I used color words, like: ☐ 2. I used number words, like:

_____   _____

_____   _____

_____   _____

☐ 3. I used shape words, like:

_____

_____

_____

My Name: _____

My Friend's Name: _____

*Use highlighters to mark any color, number, or shape words in your work!

reproducible   © Fearon Teacher Aids FE11021

c. Editing/Publishing Conference

The third type of conference takes place when a student selects his/her best writing for publication. This selection is based on how well the student has used the elements of good writing. Only those pieces that exhibit growth in writing should be selected.

To help students discuss their writing, encourage them to fill out the Writing Evaluation Chart on page 28. It also allows for self-assessment, self-selection, and the opportunity to revisit their work. You might model how to fill out this form during a mini-lesson. Begin by asking students to write only one statement. In time, move to two statements, and finally three, requiring that the entire sheet be completed before the conference. For extra guidance, place the sheets where you have posted the Elements That Promote Good Writing with student examples.

Before the conference, also suggest that students proofread and edit their pieces. An *editing checklist* might be a beneficial guide, and two are provided on pages 29 and 30.

Once the piece has been selected and edited, do a final reading with the student. Read for content, clarity, and editing. To "spice up" the rewriting process, clip or tape transparent film over the student's first draft. Then let the student use fine-tipped permanent markers to make final revisions and corrections.

The conference ends with the final draft being ready for publication. Publication processes can vary. Choose one that works best with your students, time available, resources, and classroom setting. The ultimate goal is to produce a finished product that looks polished and different from the first draft. Let time pass between publications so students can see the improvement in their writing.

Elements That Promote Good Writing

Content/Message
- inviting (grabs the reader)
- universal in appeal
- powerful

Layout/Flow
- sequence (beginning, middle, and end)
- leads (strong beginning and concluding sentences)
- order words (*first, next, then, last*)
- connecting words

Personality/Style
- humorous
- mysterious
- elements of surprise
- strong comparisons
- dialogue among characters
- side conversations with the reader

Interesting/Precise Words
- add color, spark, and sensory detail
- help the reader "picture" the story, including:
  - a. color, size, shape, and number words
  - b. "juicy" adverbs and adjectives
  - c. sensory and emotive words
  - d. "vigorous" verbs

Sentence Building and Paragraph Organizing
- super sentences/"home runs" (compound and complex)
- varied in length
- all starting in different ways
- organization of paragraph ideas

Overall Presentation
- mechanics
- usage
- grammar
- spelling

Content/Message

- I like the way you told about something that really happened to you.
- I could tell you really loved your dog. My dog died, too, so I could understand how you felt.
- What a great idea to write about when the new baby came home. The other children really seemed to understand that it took you a while to really love your new sister.

Layout/Flow

- What a great beginning sentence! You led me right in and made me "want more."
- I like the way you told me the whole story. Even your ending was powerful this time.
- Your story was so easy to follow because you had great transition words, like *before, after,* and *later.*

Personality/Style

- You did a great job with humor. Your story really made me laugh!
- Using dialogue really brought your characters to life.
- Comparing your dog to a hog (my dog is as lazy as a hog!) really gave your story more personality.
- I like the way you spoke to the reader on this page. Putting this in parentheses really helped me know that you were talking to me. (Example: "You know how princesses are.")

reproducible

Interesting/Precise Words

- I like the way you gave the word *said* a break and replaced it with words like *shouted, remarked,* and *replied.*
- Wow! This story is filled with "vigorous" verbs, like *fluttered, scampered,* and *oozed.* Those action words really helped me to picture your story in my head.
- I better understood the kind of horse you were describing when you used the word *stallion.*
- When you used the "juicy" word *greedy,* I began to predict what the old man might do next.

Sentence Building and Paragraph Organizing

- Your sentences are so much stronger in this story. You had at least three "home runs" (super sentences).
- I can see where you added more words to connect these two sentences.
- This paragraph is so much easier to read because you didn't start each sentence with *The penguin.*
- This last sentence, even though it is short, summarizes and wraps up your paragraph.

Overall Presentation

- I'm impressed that all your sentences begin with a capital letter and end with a punctuation mark.
- Wow! It's exciting to see you use quotation marks in this story.
- Most of your high-frequency (star) words are spelled correctly. You must have checked the word wall very carefully.
- You are remembering to indent each time you write a new paragraph. It really helps the reader.

Content Conference Chart

(Writing Element—Interesting Words)

Title of my story: _____

_____

My friend and I will check for interesting words.

☐ I used color words, like: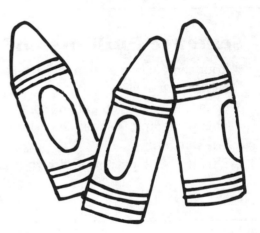

_____

_____

_____

_____

My Name: _____

My Friend's Name: _____

*Use highlighters to mark any color words in your work!

reproducible

⭐ Content Conference Chart

(Writing Element—Interesting Words)

Title of my story: _____

_____

My friend and I will check for interesting words.

☐ 1. I used color words, like: ☐ 2. I used number words, like:

_____   _____

_____   _____

_____   _____

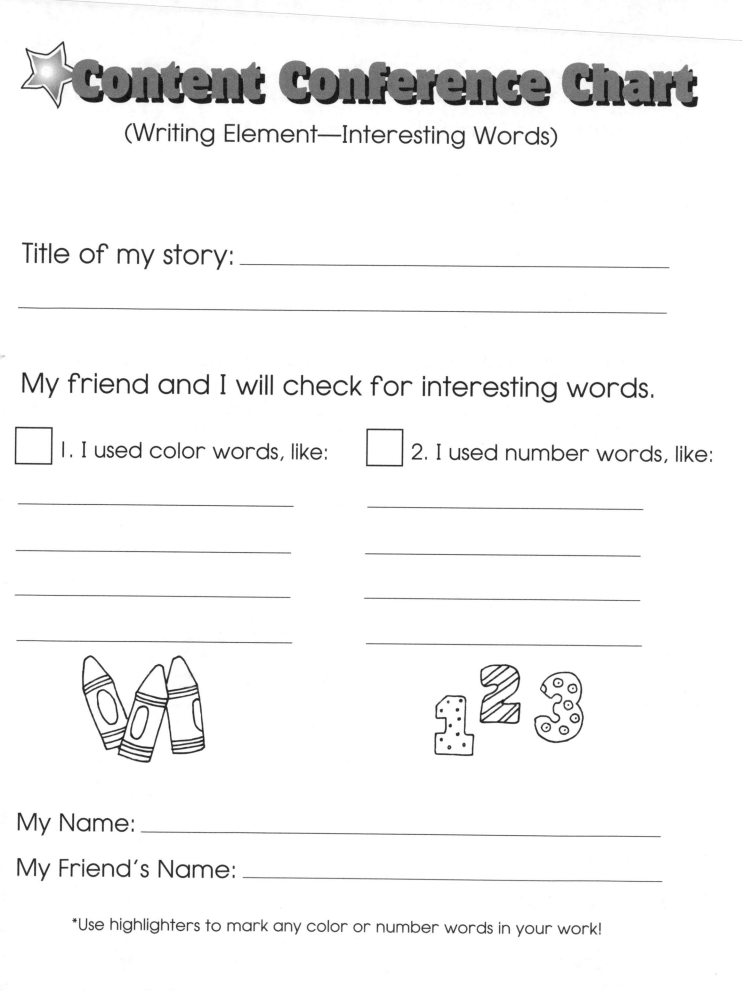

My Name: _____

My Friend's Name: _____

*Use highlighters to mark any color or number words in your work!

    reproducible

⭐ Content Conference Chart

(Writing Element—Interesting Words)

Title of my story: _____

_____

My friend and I will check for interesting words.

☐ 1. I used color words, like: ☐ 2. I used number words, like:

_____   _____

_____   _____

_____   _____

_____   _____

☐ 3. I used shape words, like:

_____

_____

_____

_____

My Name: _____

My Friend's Name: _____

*Use highlighters to mark any color, number, or shape words in your work!

    reproducible

Content Conference Chart

(Writing Element—Interesting Words)

Title of my story: _____

_____

My friend and I will check for interesting words.

☐ I used "juicy" words, like:

_____

_____

_____

_____

My Name: _____

My Friend's Name: _____

*Use highlighters to mark any "juicy" words in your work!

reproducible

Content Conference Chart

(Writing Element—Interesting Words)

Title of my story: _____

_____

My friend and I will check for interesting words.

☐ I used "vigorous" verbs, like:

_____

_____

_____

_____

My Name: _____

My Friend's Name: _____

*Use highlighters to mark any "vigorous" verbs in your work!

reproducible

Content Conference Chart

(Writing Element—Interesting Words)

Title of my story: _____

_____

My friend and I will check for words that make my writing
more interesting.

☐ 1. I used color words, like _____ and _____ .

☐ 2. I used number words, like _____ and _____ .

☐ 3. I used shape words, like _____ and _____ .

☐ 4. I used "juicy" words, like _____ and _____ .

☐ 5. I used "vigorous" verbs, like _____ and _____ .

☐ 6. I used other words for "tired" words, like *said, mad, bad,*
and *good.*

My Name: _____

My Friend's Name: _____

reproducible

Content Conference Chart

(Writing Element—Sentence Building)

Title of my story: _____

_____

I will check for these elements of good writing with my friend:

- [ ] 1. My sentences do not all begin the same way.
- [ ] 2. My friend asked me questions about my sentences.
- [ ] 3. I added more details to my sentences.
- [ ] 4. Now I have some super sentences ("home runs").

My Name: _____

My Friend's Name: _____

* Use highlighters to mark the first word in each sentence!
Highlight any "super sentences," too!

reproducible

⭐ Content Conference Chart

(Writing Element—Layout/Flow)

Title of my story: _____

_____

I will check for these elements of good writing with my friend:

☐   1. I have a good beginning sentence.

☐   2. My story has a beginning, a middle, and an end.

☐   3. The sequence of my story makes sense.

☐   4. I used words like *next, then,* and *last.*

☐   5. I have a good ending sentence.

My Name: _____

My Friend's Name: _____

* Use highlighters to show the beginning and ending sentences.
Also highlight "sequence" words, like *next, then*, and *last.*

Writing Evaluation Chart

Name: _____

Title of my story: _____

Date: _____

I think this is my best writing because:

⭐ I _____

_____

_____

_____

⭐ I also _____

_____

_____

_____

⭐ I even _____

_____

_____

_____

reproducible

Editing Chart

Name: _____

Title of my story: _____

☐ I practiced reading my story.

☐ I used capital letters and periods.

☐ I highlighted my "juicy" words.

☐ I checked the spelling of my circled words.

☐ I used my best handwriting.

reproducible

Editing Checklist

Name: _____

Title of my story: _____

☐ 1. All my sentences begin with capital letters.

☐ 2. All my sentences end with the correct punctuation. (. ? !)

☐ 3. My sentences do not all begin the same way.

☐ 4. I highlighted all my interesting words.

☐ 5. I highlighted all my connecting words.

☐ 6. I checked the spelling of any words from the word wall that I used in my writing.

reproducible © Fearon Teacher Aids FE11021

MINI-LESSONS THAT IMPROVE WRITING

⭐ Interesting/Precise Words

In teaching this particular element of good writing, you must develop in students an appreciation of authors as *artists*, as people who paint pictures in the minds of their readers. Writing must be seen as a craft, with words being the most powerful tool. If you allow students to explore the concept of word choice, you will soon see more interesting and precise words in their writing.

One effective way to instill a love of language and words is to turn the walls of your room into a giant thesaurus. Tape long sheets of paper to classroom walls, organized by category (see page 32). Categories are explored in the mini-lessons. Keep the lists posted, and encourage students to add to them.

Start your class thesaurus with "juicy" words. This term refers to interesting adjectives and adverbs, and can be introduced by challenging students to "juice up" their writing. Color words, number words, shape words, size words, overused/tired words, sensory words, and emotive words (words of emotion) all make great mini-lessons. After "juicy" words, students can explore "character" words and finally "vigorous" verbs.

The following pages provide sample lists of words. These lists are merely guides. The most meaningful lists are the ones generated by you and your students through the mini-lessons. To discover such words, invite students to examine children's literature they love and know well. After all, the words in these stories are the ones children hear in their minds. These are the words students will transfer to the lists and ultimately to their own writing.

You will notice that the mini-lessons suggested in this section are based on selections of children's literature. Do not feel that you must use these exact books. Rather, look closely at the strategies of each lesson. *The strategies are the key.* They are transferable to any piece of children's literature you and your students choose.

The mini-lessons are divided into five specific types of words that primary students can easily weave into their writing:

1. Color/number/size and shape words
2. Character traits
3. Overused/tired words
4. Sensory/emotive words
5. "Vigorous" verbs

Tip! When adding words to the classroom thesaurus, instruct students to write the words on self-stick notes when they find them, then to place the notes on the appropriate lists. You might discuss the new words with the class, then write the words permanently on the list. This way, your lists will remain neat and readable.

 Tip! If wall space is a problem, you could display only that list of words on which your mini-lesson is focused. Once students become somewhat proficient with those words, transfer them to a special Word Choice Big Book. Keep the book in the class writing center.

Interesting/Precise Word Lists

Shape Words

fat	wide
thin	tall
round	curly
pointy	spiked
skinny	swollen
long	broken
short	

Number Words

1. one
2. two
3. three
4. four
5. five
6. six
7. seven
8. eight
9. nine
10. ten

Color Words

red
blue
green
purple
brown
orange
black
yellow

"Juicy" Words

big	spotted
large	small
enormous	dark
greedy	stormy
shy	shiny
strong	tiny

Active or "Vigorous" Verbs

horses	THUNDER
volcanoes	ERUPT
fireworks	EXPLODE
lions	POUNCE
sharks	CHOMP
tigers	ROAR
monkeys	SCREECH
coyotes	HOWL

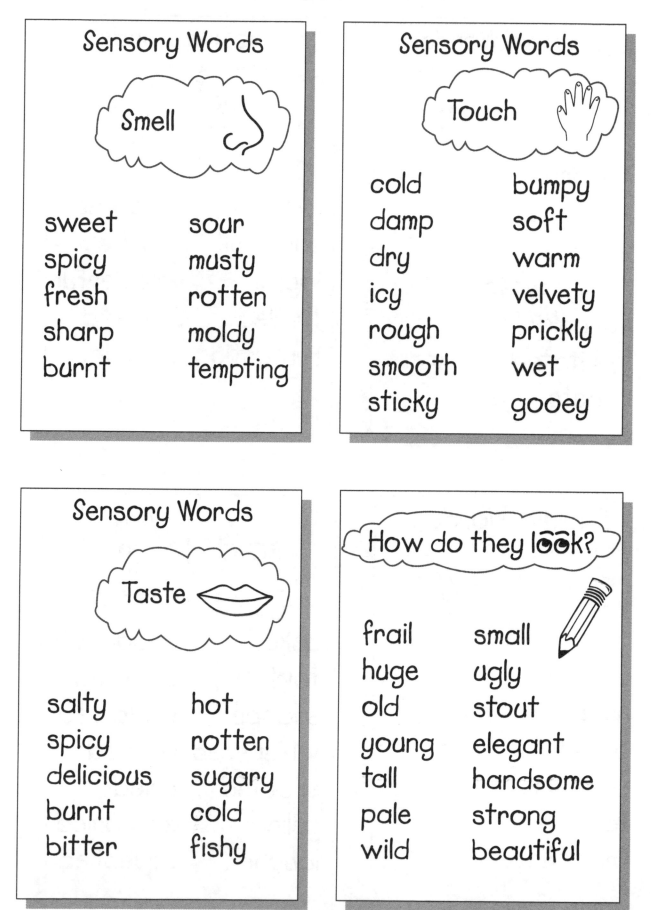

Sensory Words

Smell

sweet	sour
spicy	musty
fresh	rotten
sharp	moldy
burnt	tempting

Sensory Words

Touch

cold	bumpy
damp	soft
dry	warm
icy	velvety
rough	prickly
smooth	wet
sticky	gooey

Sensory Words

Taste

salty	hot
spicy	rotten
delicious	sugary
burnt	cold
bitter	fishy

How do they look?

frail	small
huge	ugly
old	stout
young	elegant
tall	handsome
pale	strong
wild	beautiful

Emotive Words

mad

angry
annoyed
cross
aggravated
cranky
irritated
nasty

Emotive Words

happy

glad   delighted
cheerful   terrific
joyful   wonderful
thrilled   splendid
fantastic   marvelous

Emotive Words

bad

dreadful
horrible
awful
appalling
terrible
frightful

said

I'm so tired!

asked   groaned
told   ordered
snapped   exclaimed
whispered   roared
shouted   cried
yelled   screamed
laughed   squeaked

~~~~~~

Describing Feature: Color, Number, and Size

(WRITING ELEMENT—INTERESTING/PRECISE WORDS)

For your first mini-lesson, choose a book that coincides with a learning theme you and your students are currently investigating. The book may even be one with which students are already familiar. In this way, the book is revisited and explored more fully. For example, if your class is learning about the ocean, *The Greedy Gray Octopus* by Christel Buckley wonderfully connects sea life with writing and word choice.

What to Do:

1. Gather the class in your reading corner and display the book. Share with children that authors use special words when they write to help us, the readers, picture the stories in our minds. These special words also make the writing more exciting. These words can be called "juicy" words because they "juice up" a story. To show children what you mean, place highlighter tape over the words *greedy* and *gray* on the book cover and title page. Have students notice these words, pointing out that without them, the book would be called simply *The Octopus*. Talk about how these words "juice up" the book title.

"Juicy" Words	Color Words
greedy	gray
big	blue
juicy	green
bright	red
shiny	silver
	black

2. Begin to read the story with the class. Ask students to raise their hands each time they hear a word that makes the character easy to imagine or more exciting. Read each page slowly, pointing to each word as you read it, and allowing time for students to appreciate the precise wording. Before moving on to the next page, invite a student to come to the book and cover the "juicy" words with highlighter tape.

3. For further emphasis, reread the story, this time leaving out all the "juicy" words. Then take a class vote—*Which version of the story is more interesting to read? Why?* Help students conclude that the "juicy" words are an important writing element added by the author.

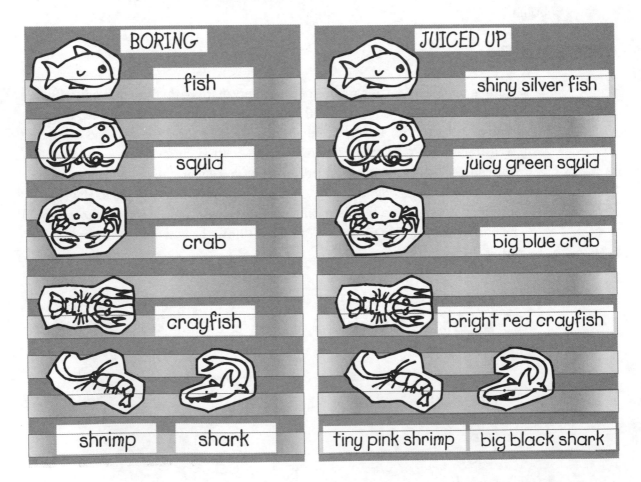

© Fearon Teacher Aids FE11021

Describing Feature: Color, Number, and Size

(WRITING ELEMENT–INTERESTING/PRECISE WORDS)

The following day, invite students to explore the book again with this pocket-chart activity. Encourage them to notice how word choice "juices up" a story. Remember—the activity can be modified to fit any book. *The Greedy Gray Octopus* is only an example.

What to Do:

1. Ahead of time, draw a picture for each character in the story. You might let volunteers help with this task. Also, create sentence strips for your pocket chart. Sentences should include the character's name, along with describing words found in the text. Fold each sentence strip so the describing words are hidden.
2. Invite the class to the pocket chart. Begin to reread the book.
3. When children meet each character, place the character's picture in the pocket chart. Place the folded sentence strip next to the picture. Have students read the words. Follow their reading with the word *boring!*
4. Ask a child to come to the pocket chart and unfold the strip. Now have students read the description again, this time following their reading with the word *juicy!*
5. Continue in this way with the other characters.
6. After reading, use the words in the pocket chart to generate your first word list for your classroom thesaurus. Point out any patterns in the author's writing. (For example, in *The Greedy Gray Octopus*, the author writes a "juicy" word, followed by a color word.) Suggest that children separate their words into specific lists, such as "juicy" words and color words.

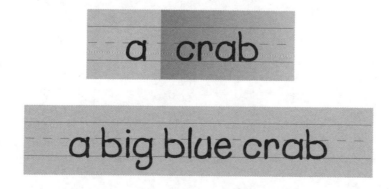

Describing Feature: Color, Number, and Size

(WRITING ELEMENT—INTERESTING/PRECISE WORDS)

Further sharpen children's awareness and appreciation of "juicy" words by encouraging them to explore other books. A great source of interesting/precise word examples can be found in *Where Do Monsters Live?* by Rozanne Lanczak Williams, from which the following mini-lesson is derived.

What to Do:

1. Gather students into your reading corner, and present the book *Where Do Monsters Live?* Over the next two days, have them explore the book in the same manner as *The Greedy Gray Octopus*, following the directions for Mini-Lessons 1 and 2.

2. If time allows, lead students to find other words to add to the classroom thesaurus as they enjoy other books with a monster theme, such as *What Do You See?*, *Five Little Monsters*, and *Ten Monsters in a Bed*, all by Rozanne Lanczak Williams, along with *The Monster Under My Bed* by Suzanne Gruber.

3. Now that students have had adequate instruction in recognizing interesting/precise words, send them off in pairs to reread other favorite books in your classroom library. Supply them with self-stick notes on which to write down any color, shape, or size words, or other "juicy" describing words they find.

4. After partners have explored their books, let students share, round-table style, some of their words. Have students place their notes on your classroom thesaurus lists. (Sample lists shown below.)

Color Words		Number Words		"Juicy" Words	
gray	black	ten	10	greedy	round
blue	purple	nine	9	big	dark
green	orange	eight	8	juicy	scary
red	pink	seven	7	bright	spooky
silver		six	6	shiny	wicked
		five	5	striped	hairy
		four	4	spotted	fluffy
		three	3	invisible	fuzzy
		two	2	furry	
		one	1		

Describing Feature: Color, Number, and Size

(WRITING ELEMENT–INTERESTING/PRECISE WORDS)

Now that students have explored a variety of books and have recognized interesting/precise words, invite them to practice word choice in their own writing. For this mini-lesson, children will look closely at the writing of one of their classmates. Therefore, prompt students to write their own stories. Make the stories meaningful by tying them to a theme your class is studying, such as oceans or monsters, as suggested in the previous mini-lessons.

What to Do:

1. Once the stories have been written, choose one story for the mini-lesson. Be sure to select a story that includes color words, number words, "juicy" words, and/or other interesting/precise words featured in the previous mini-lessons. So the entire class can view the story, transcribe the story onto transparencies for the overhead.
2. Invite the student author to come to the overhead and lead the class in reading his or her story.
3. Ask the class to assist the author in finding interesting/precise words in the story. If this is the first time children are reading a classmate's work, it might be best to have children look for one type of word, such as color words. If children are asked to find too much, they may feel over-challenged and become discouraged. Have the author highlight color words found in the story.

Describing Feature: Color, Number, and Size

(WRITING ELEMENT–INTERESTING/PRECISE WORDS)

Now that students have written their own stories and had practice examining a classmate's story up close, let them work together in conferencing sessions. Peer conferencing will take two sessions.

What to Do:

1. Before children conference, introduce and model how to use the Content Conference Chart. Remember to choose a sheet that is specific to words being taught in the mini-lessons.
2. Assign students to partners. Tell partners to choose one of their stories, then supply them with highlighters. Instruct student pairs to read the story together, highlighting the interesting words they find. Be sure students take turns highlighting so that it is a learning experience for both. Circulate among the class to get a feel for how well children understand the concept.
3. Tell partners to fill in the Content Conference Chart. Then have them clip or staple the sheet to the story.
4. The next day, have children work with the same partners to read the other student's writing, following the same procedure. You might share your observations from the previous day to guide the process, perhaps displaying examples of highlighted stories.
5. Once peer-conferencing sessions are finished, gather the class and discuss the words students have written on the Content Conference Chart. Let them check the classroom thesaurus for any new words that can be added.

Content Conference Chart
(Writing Element—Interesting Words)

Title of my story: Monsters at skul

My friend and I will check for interesting words.

☑ I used color words, like:
red
green
purple

My Name: Lisa
My Friend's Name: Mrs. K

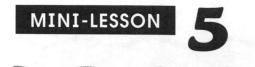

Describing Feature: Color, Number, and Size

(WRITING ELEMENT–INTERESTING/PRECISE WORDS)

Now is the perfect time to encourage children to improve their stories.

What to Do:

1. Have students take out their stories, and ask volunteers to share sentences that did not have any interesting/precise words in them. Ask permission to write down the sentences to use in a mini-lesson.
2. Then write the sentence with the child's name next to it on a sentence strip. Place the strips in your pocket chart.
3. Reread the sentences with the class. Brainstorm with children color words, number words, "juicy" words, or other interesting/precise words that could "juice up" the sentences. Depending on the level of your class, you might only focus on one type of word.
4. Suggest that students view the class thesaurus lists around the room for words to add to the sentences. Have students or partners write appropriate words for the sentences on sentence strips.
5. Then invite the authors of the sentences to the pocket chart. Help children cut apart the sentences, then slip in the "juicy" words suggested by classmates.
6. With the class, reread the new sentences. Talk about how word choice plays an important role in making the sentences more exciting.

 Tip! Encourage children to write their interesting/precise words in bright colors. This way, "juicy" words will stand out. This mini-lesson also makes a great pocket-chart activity for center time.

Describing Feature: Color, Number, and Size

(WRITING ELEMENT–INTERESTING/PRECISE WORDS)

Many primary students, especially those in second and third grade, are ready to add more than just the basic color words to their writing. They are often fascinated by precise words, like *maroon* or *crimson* or even *razzmatazz red*. This fun, cooperative mini-lesson challenges children with this puzzling question: *Well, how red was it?*

What to Do:

1. Ahead of time, divide a jumbo box of crayons into the following color groups: red, blue, green, yellow, brown, orange, pink, and purple. You will need at least 100 crayons. Place each color group in a separate see-through plastic baggie. Put all eight baggies in a special box or tin. Decorate the container with jazzy colors and the title *Razzmatazz It!*

2. Also put together a class book. You will need eight sheets of white construction paper and eight sheets of tagboard, each measuring 12" x 18" (30.5 cm x 45.5 cm). Glue the construction paper to the tagboard for durability. Cut a tag for each page, write one color on it, and glue it to the side of the page. The tabs should be staggered on the sides so children can read all of them.

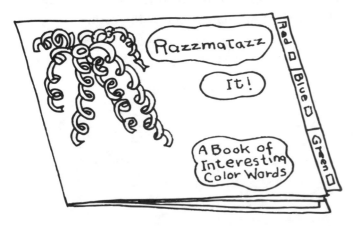

3. At the top of each page, write the question, *Well, how [color] was it?* Add numbered writing lines to each page for students to write on. At the end of each writing line, draw large squares. Children will color in these squares with the appropriate crayons.

4. Gather the children around you, and present them with the *Razzmatazz It!* box. Shake it and speculate what is inside. *What do they think* razzmatazz *means? How might it relate to their writing?* Guide students to figure out that *razzmatazz* is another way of saying, "Juice it up!"

5. Open the box and take out the baggies of crayons. Ask students for color words to describe the crayons in each bag. Record their words on chart paper. Point out that each color has variations. Remind them that good writers use precise language to help readers more accurately picture colors and other things.

6. To show children what you mean, present these examples:

   From Sylvester and the Magic Pebble *by William Steig:*
   When describing Sylvester's magic stone, the author paints the picture that the stone is "flaming red, shiny, and perfectly round."
   How red was it? (flaming red)

   From The Courage of Sarah Noble *by Alice Dalgliesh:*
   When describing Sarah's house in the fall, the author paints the picture: "The trees had put on their finest scarlet."
   How red was it? (scarlet red)

   Write the words *flaming red* and *scarlet* next to the word *red* on your chart list.

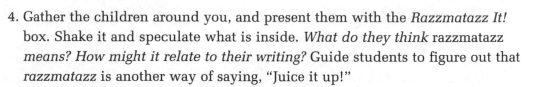

7. Point out to students that when writing, it is important to let the reader know specifically how red, blue, green, yellow, or brown something is. Then ask students to take an oath, or promise, that they will try very hard not to break. They will promise that they will try to use more precise colors words in their writing from now on.

8. Write the oath, as shown, on 12" x 18" (30.5 cm x 45.5 cm) paper as children read it with you. Have children write their names below the oath.

We do solemnly swear, from this day forward, to only use interesting color words in our writing.

Sarah	April
Emilee	Keith
John	Tim
Da Shauna	Dianna
Travon	Lee
William	Chris
Kerry	Jeffrey
Marc	Scott

9. Glue the oath to the inside front cover of the *Razzmatazz It!* book, then hold up the book for the class to see. Show children the format of each page, pointing out that a page has been made for each color in a group of crayons.

10. Now divide the class into color groups. Give each group a baggie of crayons and the matching page from the book. Encourage children to take out their crayons and talk about the color. *What fun words can they think of to describe it? What interesting/precise words would more aptly describe its color? What is the name of this color on the crayon?* Have children write the names on scrap paper.

11. Meet informally with each group and review their words. Help them correct any misspellings.

12. Then let children write their final color words on their *Razzmatazz It!* book page.

13. Invite each group to share its page of color words with the class.

14. Then assemble the pages, or invite a group of volunteers to put the pages of the book together.

15. Keep the book in your writing center. Remind children to check the book when writing so they can *razzmatazz* their color words!

Tip! After this exercise, hopefully students will start to look at color words more closely when they read stories on their own. If so, encourage them to write new color words they discover on self-stick notes, and to place the notes on the appropriate pages of the class book. When many new words have been added, review them with the class, then write them in the book.

Sample Inside Pages from *Rassmatazz It!* Class Book

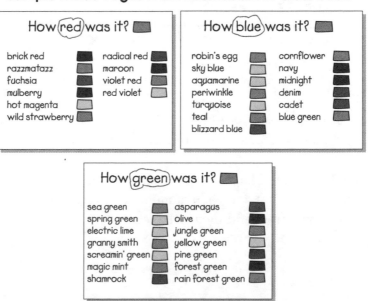

How (red) was it?

brick red	radical red
razzmatazz	maroon
fuchsia	violet red
mulberry	red violet
hot magenta	
wild strawberry	

How (blue) was it?

robin's egg	cornflower
sky blue	navy
aquamarine	midnight
periwinkle	denim
turquoise	cadet
teal	blue green
blizzard blue	

How (green) was it?

sea green	asparagus
spring green	olive
electric lime	jungle green
granny smith	yellow green
screamin' green	pine green
magic mint	forest green
shamrock	rain forest green

Character Traits

(WRITING ELEMENT—INTERESTING/PRECISE WORDS)

In order to make their stories more powerful, young writers need to look at character development. They need to learn how to create strong characters who exhibit specific traits. Such developed traits make story characters like Charlotte in *Charlotte's Web* and Lilly in *Lilly's Purple Plastic Purse* endearing to readers. Begin by examining story characters who children already know and love.

What to Do:

1. Invite children to select favorite books from the class library to bring to the reading corner. Collect the books and talk with children about why they like them. List children's ideas on chart paper. After a moment, pause and point out the characters children have listed as reasons why they enjoy these books.

2. Then talk about the characters more specifically. On a fresh sheet of chart paper, model a describing sentence about the characters. The sentences should include a character trait as well as a justification for that trait. For example:

> The **little boy** was **kind** because he let the nightmare sleep in his bed. (*There's a Nightmare in My Closet* by Mercer Mayer)
>
> **Somebody** was very **mischievous** because he really made a mess of the Blairs' house. (*Somebody and the Three Blairs* by Marilyn Tolhurst)
>
> **Big Anthony** was **disobedient** because he touched the pasta pot. (*Strega Nona* by Tomie de Paola)
>
> **Froggy** was **embarrassed** because he forgot his underwear. (*Froggy Gets Dressed* by Jonathan London)
>
> **Alexander** was **frustrated** because he was having a bad day. (*Alexander and the Terrible, Horrible, No Good, Very Bad Day* by Judith Viorst)
>
> **Lilly** was **impatient** because she wanted everyone to see her purse right away. (*Lilly's Purple Plastic Purse* by Kevin Henkes)

3. After these close-up examinations, help children conclude that *traits* are what make a character interesting to read about.

 Tip! This type of language may not come easily to children. You may have to lead frequently at first, but soon students will meet characters who have traits they've already explored, and they will be able to identify the traits on their own.

© Fearon Teacher Aids FE11021

Character Traits

(WRITING ELEMENT–INTERESTING/PRECISE WORDS)

Sample Book Cover

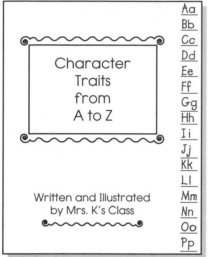

| Aa |
| Bb |
| Cc |
| Dd |
| Ee |
| Ff |
| Gg |
| Hh |
| Ii |
| Jj |
| Kk |
| Ll |
| Mm |
| Nn |
| Oo |
| Pp |

Invite children to write their own sentences that tell about a character's traits. They will add these sentences, along with drawings, to a class book titled *Character Traits from A to Z.*

What to Do:

1. Share with children that they are going to make a class book about their favorite story characters. The book will be arranged in alphabetical order, not according to character name, but according to character trait. For example, Lilly from *Lilly's Purple Plastic Purse* would be found under *I* for *impatient*, Lilly's character trait.

2. Let students work with classmates that have the same favorite book or character. Encourage partners to talk about the character, brainstorming words that describe the character's personality. Tell them to come up with one word that fits the character overall. On scrap paper, challenge partners to compose a describing sentence, as modeled in Mini-Lesson 7.

Sample Pages for "Cc" Traits

Swimmy was clever because he got all the little fish to make a big fish.

Rainbow fish was conceited because she thought she was the most beautiful fish of all.

Jerome was cagey because he knew how to trick the Gatorman Kids.

Sarah Noble was courageous because she stayed alone in the wilderness.

3. Have partners reread the sentence for misspellings and make any corrections. Then tell one student to rewrite the sentence on fresh paper, while the other student draws a picture of the character in a picture frame. (See page 48 for frame patterns.)

4. Invite pairs to share their sentences with the class. Then compile the sentences in a class book, arranged alphabetically (see examples on left). Instruct children to glue the sentences on one page, and the pictures on another. Spread out the readings over several days/mini-lessons.

5. Add to the *Character Traits from A to Z* book throughout the year as students meet new book characters.

Character Trait Picture Frames

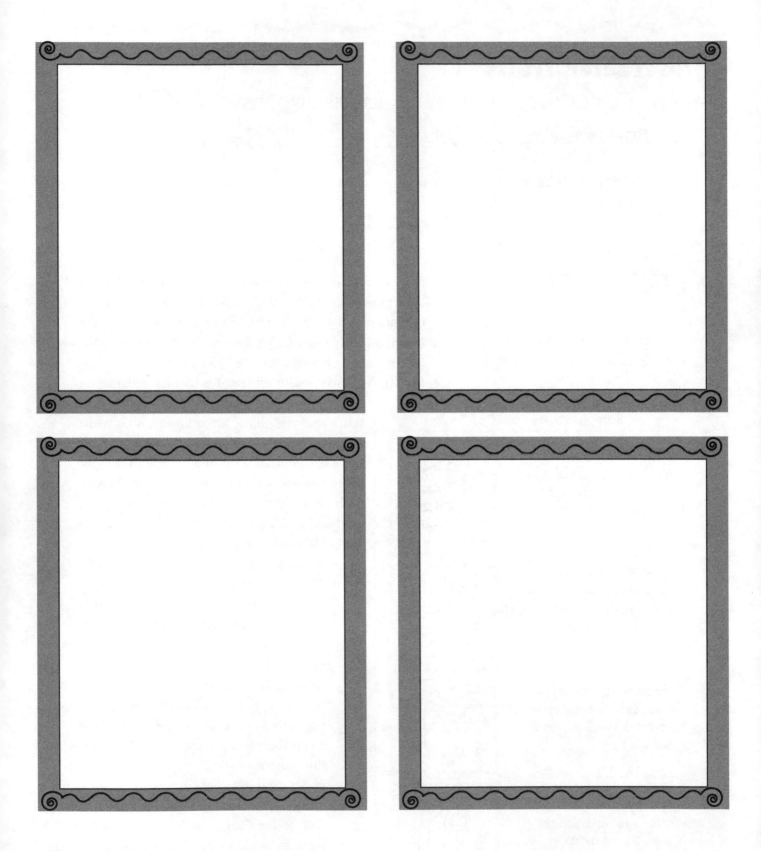

reproducible

Character Traits: Names

(WRITING ELEMENT–INTERESTING/PRECISE WORDS)

Now that students have become involved with characters and their personalities, encourage children to examine the power of character names. A character becomes more developed when given a name that reflects his or her traits.

What to Do:

1. Ahead of time, get a copy of *The Old Man's Mitten* by Yevonne Pollock. Create a picture for each animal character. (Animal cards you have for another project can work, too; the animals don't need to look exactly like those in the book.) You will also need a pocket chart, a large mitten, and paper strips, each bearing the description of one character. Place the strips in the mitten.

2. Then gather the class to the reading corner and display the book. Set up the character pictures along a chalkboard or easel ledge. Begin to read.

3. Each time a new character is introduced, invite a volunteer to find his or her picture and place it in the pocket chart.

4. After reading, tell children that they are going to play the Name Game. Hold up the mitten and encourage a student to reach in and pull out a paper strip. Have the student read the strip aloud. Challenge the class to match the descriptive words on the strip with the character picture in the pocket chart.

5. Continue until all the characters and names have been matched. Then review the pocket chart, pointing out that the characters' names are actually fun, descriptive words that tell about the character.

Character Traits: Names

(WRITING ELEMENT–INTERESTING/PRECISE WORDS)

Continue exploring character names with children by reading *Snap!* by Marcia Vaughan.

What to Do:

1. As with the previous mini-lesson, obtain a copy of the book and create pictures for the characters featured in the story.
2. Gather the class at the reading corner. Display the book, along with a pocket chart and the character drawings. Share with children that as they read and listen to the story, you want them to pay special attention to the characters' names.
3. Read the book through once so children become familiar with the story and characters.
4. Then visit the book again. Stop on each page when a new character is introduced. Invite a student to find the picture of that character and place it in the pocket chart.
5. Then talk with students about the character's name. *What trait does the character have? How does his or her name reflect that trait?*
6. Ask a student to write the name on a strip for the pocket chart, while another student writes the type of animal on a second strip. Have students use different-colored markers for each.
7. Let students place the names in the pocket chart. The sequence for each character should be: picture-character, name-type of animal.
8. Encourage students to come to the pocket chart and ask them to look at the picture of the character. Using a grease pencil or dry-erase marker, have students circle the physical feature on which the character's name is based.

Character Traits: Names

(WRITING ELEMENT–INTERESTING/PRECISE WORDS)

Now that students have become familiar with the ways in which some authors name their characters to reflect character traits, invite children to come up with fun character names of their own.

What to Do:

1. Ahead of time, reproduce the Animal Picture Cards from page 52 and the Writing Cards from page 53. Cut apart the Animal Picture Cards. Make sure you have enough cards for half the students in your class.

2. Buddy up the students, and give each pair one animal picture card and a set of writing cards.

Clever Character Names

Picture	Animal Name	Feature Name
	squirrel	Big Bushy Tail
	shark	Sharp-tooth
	kangaroo	Big Feet
	jaguar	Spotty
	elephant	Trumpeter
	rabbit	Hoppity-Hop

3. Challenge partners to come up with clever names for their animals that reflect a physical feature they see on the animal picture card. Instruct them to write the fun, made-up name on a writing card. On a second writing card, have them write the actual animal name. For example, for the kangaroo, the words *Big Feet* would be on one card (physical feature), and the word *kangaroo* would be on the other (actual animal name).

4. Invite children to color their animal cards and circle the physical features that helped them come up with the character names.

5. When ready, invite partners to share their character names with the class. Challenge the rest of the class to figure out to which animal the name belongs.

6. As partners finish, have them glue their animal cards and name cards to a wall-sized chart titled *Clever Character Names*. Tell children to try to use clever names like these when writing their own stories.

Animal Picture Cards

squirrel	butterfly
zebra	giraffe
monkey	elephant
rabbit	jaguar
kangaroo	shark

reproducible

Writing Cards

Overused/Tired Words: Said

(WRITING ELEMENT–INTERESTING/PRECISE WORDS)

It's a simple fact: Beginning writers often use certain words over and over and over again. These words become exhausted, and the only thing to be done is to encourage children to give these words a rest. The following mini-lessons suggest ways to do this.

What to Do:

1. Ahead of time, create a large outline of a bed. You might enlarge the bed pattern on page 56. Look through your class library for a favorite book that uses the word *said* over and over again. To provide examples, this mini-lesson focuses on *Ten Monsters in a Bed* by Rozanne Lanczak Williams.

2. Invite children to the reading center. Tell them you have noticed that the word *said* appears over and over again in their stories. When a word is used as frequently as *said*, it becomes very tired. It's time for us to give *said* a break. Let's send *said* to bed and find other words to replace it.

3. With children, begin to read the book you have selected. Each time children hear the word *said*, invite them to raise their hands. Select a child to place a piece of highlighter tape over the word *said*.

4. After reading, review all the pieces of tape. Pretend to be sad that *said* must be so tired by now.

5. Then begin to write *said* sentences from the story on strips for the pocket chart as students draw pictures of the characters from the story. For example, if you are reading *Ten Monsters in a Bed*, you could have pictures for the mad one, the sad one, the funny one, and the shy one. The sentences on your strips would be:

    The **mad** one **said,** "Roll over, roll over!"
    The **sad** one **said,** "Roll over, roll over!"
    The **funny** one **said,** "Roll over, roll over!"
    The **shy** one **said,** "Roll over, roll over!"

Be sure to write the name of each character in a different color from the word *said*. Place the sentence strips in the pocket chart, along with children's drawings.

6. As children read each sentence, invite several students to pantomime the emotion. For example, *how might the mad one act? the sad one? the funny one? the shy one?* Hopefully, the demonstration will generate ideas for a word other than *said*. Guide students to that conclusion; for example, the mad one might *roar*.

7. Tell children it is time to put *said* to bed. Remove the sentence strip from the pocket chart, and ask a student to cut away the word *said*. Have the student tape the word *said* to the bed picture.

8. Now write the new word on another strip, and invite a child to place the new word in the sentence. Read the new sentence with the class.

9. Continue until all the *said*s have been put to bed and new words have been added. For example:

> The **mad** one **roared,** "Roll over, roll over!"
> The **sad** one **cried,** "Roll over, roll over!"
> The **funny** one **laughed,** "Roll over, roll over!"
> The **shy** one **whispered,** "Roll over, roll over!"

Put <u>Said</u> to Bed!

56

reproducible

© Fearon Teacher Aids FE11021

Put Said to Bed!

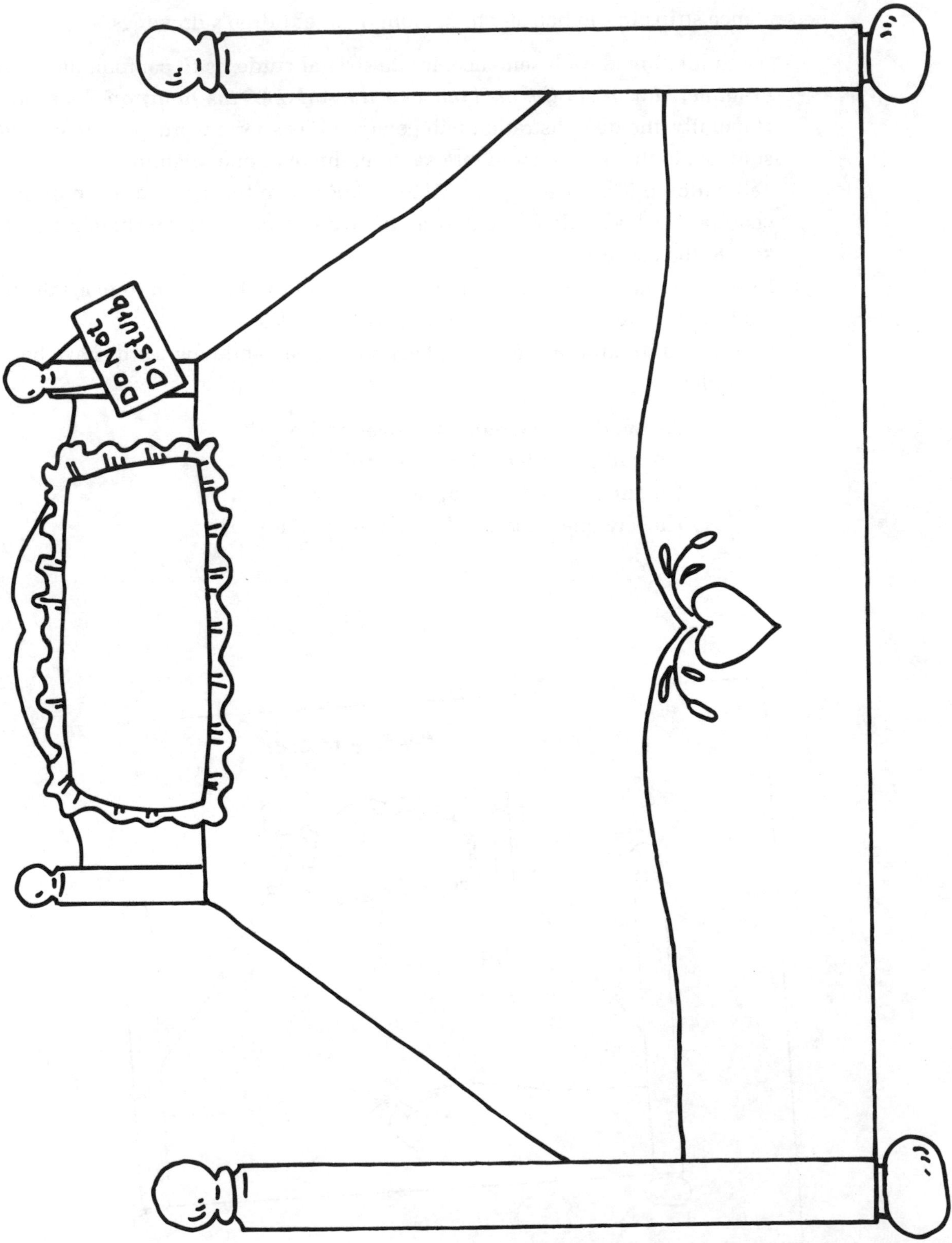
Do Not
Disturb

Overused/Tired Words: Said

(WRITING ELEMENT–INTERESTING/PRECISE WORDS)

Invite students to call upon their favorite book characters to discover other words to use for *said*.

What to Do:

1. Ahead of time, go through a selection of children's favorite books. Look through the books for words the authors used instead of *said*. Mark these book pages with bright-colored self-stick notes. Put the books back in your reading section, preferably in a section designated as class favorites.

2. Invite children to the class library to select their favorite books to bring to the reading corner. Begin by talking with children about the word *said*. Remind them that they have been putting *said* to bed, and indicate the bed outline. Suggest that in today's lesson, they ask their favorite book characters for other words to use for *said*.

3. Ask students who have books with bright-colored self-stick notes to turn to marked pages. Talk about each book separately. Have the child bring the book to you, then read the sentence aloud. Encourage children to listen carefully to the conversation, or words of dialogue, for any words other than *said*.

4. Display a sheet of chart paper. Write the book title across the top, then write the sentence of dialogue. Invite a student to the chart to highlight the word in the sentence that has been used instead of *said*. (You might also take this opportunity to review quotation marks.)

5. Repeat this process with the other marked books children have brought to the reading center.

6. Close the lesson by inviting students to become "word detectives" in search of more ways to keep *said* in bed. Suggest that when they find good replacement words for *said*, they should write the words on self-stick notes to add to the chart.

Tip! Record the replacement words for *said* on cards for your pocket chart. Invite students to then use the words in sentences. Be sure to include a sample sentence at the top of the pocket chart, and remind students that dialogue in their stories needs quotation marks.

Words to Use Instead of *Said:*

gasped	squealed	barked
replied	squeaked	chirped
trumpeted	groaned	whined
shouted	whispered	complained
yelled	crooned	whistled
exclaimed	babbled	hooted
spoke	bellowed	laughed
asked	croaked	persisted
cried	bleated	bawled
called	answered	challenged
sighed	added	declared
hissed	hollered	suggested
sang	shrieked	rumbled
yawned	cheered	pleaded
moaned	told	sobbed
	screamed	guffawed

The following books contain great replacement words for *said:*

Froggy Gets Dressed by Jonathan London
Rainbow Fish by Marcus Pfister
The Wide-Mouthed Frog by Keith Faulkner
Snap! by Marcia Vaughan
Gotcha! by Kerry Argent
Five Little Monsters by Rozanne Lanczak
 Williams
The Old Man's Mitten by Yevonne Pollock

The following sentences were generated by primary students after working on replacement words for *said:*

"I found a stray dog," exclaimed Missy.

"Don't forget to pay me!" called the man.

"I'm on a chain!" bleated the lamb.

"Get in line," complained Mrs. Vance.

"I've touched a fluffy rabbit," gasped Cyril.

"We will be there forever!" exclaimed Carrie.

"Yes, I have a wife," answered Mr. Canales.

MINI-LESSON **14**

Overused/Tired Words: Bad

(WRITING ELEMENT–INTERESTING/PRECISE WORDS)

Which other words do children overuse in their writing? Stretch children's vocabularies by discovering other words for *bad*.

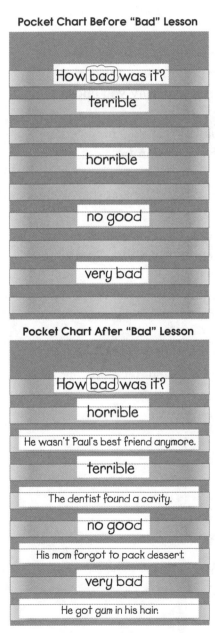

Pocket Chart Before "Bad" Lesson

How (bad) was it?
terrible
horrible
no good
very bad

Pocket Chart After "Bad" Lesson

How (bad) was it?
horrible
He wasn't Paul's best friend anymore.
terrible
The dentist found a cavity.
no good
His mom forgot to pack dessert.
very bad
He got gum in his hair.

What to Do:

1. Ahead of time, obtain a copy of *Alexander and the Terrible, Horrible, No Good, Very Bad Day* by Judith Viorst. Write events from the book on separate sentence strips for your pocket chart. On other strips, write *terrible, horrible, no good,* and *very bad*.

2. Now gather the class in the reading center. Hold up the bed with the word *said* (page 56), and explain that it is time for *said* to roll over. Invite a volunteer to move the note to one side of the bed.

3. Then mention that you have noticed that children use the word *bad* a lot. It is now time to put *bad* to bed.

4. Hold up the book *Alexander and the Terrible, Horrible, No Good, Very Bad Day*. Read the title to the class. *What do they think* terrible *and* horrible *mean?* They also mean "bad."

5. Read the book with the class. Then discuss the events that made Alexander's day so bad. Hold up a sentence strip for one event. *How bad was it?* Let children vote on whether the event was terrible, horrible, no good, or just very bad. Have a student place the sentence strip for the event in the pocket chart, along with the "bad" word children have chosen. Ask other students to write the word *bad* on notes to place in the bed outline.

Overused/Tired Words: Bad

(WRITING ELEMENT–INTERESTING/PRECISE WORDS)

Continue to encourage children to put *bad* to bed with this follow-up mini-lesson that draws from the children's book *What If?* by A. H. Benjamin.

What to Do:

1. Invite children to your reading center, and present the book *What If?* Explain that as you read this book, children are going to hear words they can use in their writing. Instruct children to listen carefully to figure out why you chose this book.

2. Begin to read. It shouldn't take long before students realize that the characters express how "bad" things are on a farm in a variety of ways. Stop for a moment, and say, "Yes! You're right! This book will help us find replacement words for *bad!* When we finish, we'll go back and take a closer look at the language the author used."

3. Continue reading. Afterward, briefly discuss the plot, as well as the emotions expressed by the characters. If time permits, let children buddy up to share their favorite parts.

4. Then go through the book, page by page, and point out the large bold print that represents what might happen if a kangaroo came to the farm. Invite students to place highlighter tape over the sentences.

5. Close the book, and challenge students to recall all the words for *bad* from the story. If you discussed Alexander from the previous mini-lesson, let children include those words, too. Record their responses on chart paper.

Other Ways to Say *Bad*

dreadful	no good
horrible	unfortunate
awful	outrageous
appalling	unacceptable
terrible	frightful

Emotive and Sensory Words: Sense of Touch

(WRITING ELEMENT–INTERESTING/PRECISE WORDS)

Young authors in training also need to learn how to choose specific words that appeal to the emotions and senses of the reader. These adjectives and adverbs are called sensory and emotive words. *Sensory words* are taught and categorized by the *five senses*. *Emotive words* are taught and categorized by *feelings*. Since most primary students are exposed to science and/or social studies lessons that deal with the five senses and recognizing emotions, they can easily learn to add these words to their writing. The following mini-lessons examine these words in stories that may be familiar to students. As before, a book is suggested to guide the lesson, but feel free to use another book that is appropriate and available to your class.

What to Do:

1. Choose a book that features a child exploring the sense of touch. One effective book is *I Can't Sleep* by Kimberlee Graves. In this story, a young boy has trouble falling asleep because he keeps feeling things in his bed.
2. Prepare by writing adjectives that describe what the boy (or other character) feels, such as *hard, bumpy, lumpy,* and *sticky,* on word cards to fit in your pocket chart.
3. To get children thinking about their sense of touch, you might also prepare several bags of "mystery" objects, one for each description. For example, something hard (wooden block), something bumpy (bubble wrap), something lumpy (baggie filled with rubber balls), and something sticky (sticker).
4. Gather children to the reading center and present them with the mystery bags. Invite volunteers to place their hands in the bags, describe what they feel, then predict what's inside. Point out that students are relying on their sense of touch to solve the mystery.
5. Recall with children that we learn things through our five senses, and challenge them to recall each sense (seeing, hearing, touching, tasting, and smelling). Cut out the pictures on page 65, and place them in your pocket chart.
6. Mention to children that good authors often include words that describe the five senses, or sensory words, in their stories. These words help the reader imagine what is happening.

7. Present the book *I Can't Sleep*. Read the story with the class. Then ask children which sense is most prominent in the story. Invite a student to come to the pocket chart and remove the hand.

8. On a table or ledge, spread out the word cards you created earlier. As you hold the hand cutout, invite children to reread the story, this time paying special attention to words that describe how something feels when we touch it. Pause after each word, invite a child to the table to find the word, then place the word in the pocket chart.

9. Finally, discuss with students the objects the boy found in his bed. Brainstorm other objects that the boy could have found. For example, on page five, the little boy feels something bumpy. It turns out to be a bag of marbles. *What else could the bumpy thing have been?* Let students have fun exploring suitable substitutes, giving children the opportunity to orally practice these sensory words.

Emotive and Sensory Words: Sense of Touch

(WRITING ELEMENT–INTERESTING/PRECISE WORDS)

Invite children to help you compose lists of adjectives to describe how things feel, sound, taste, smell, and look for a class big book of sensory words.

Sample Cover

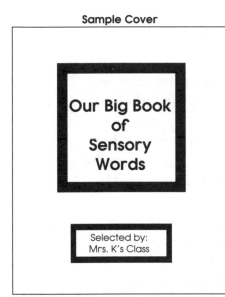

Our Big Book
of
Sensory
Words

Selected by:
Mrs. K's Class

What to Do:

1. Ahead of time, create a big book in which children can record sensory words. Get a large sheet of poster paper, and attach five pages of chart paper to it. The cover and the pages should all be the same size. Write a title for the big book, such as *Our Big Book of Sensory Words*. Be sure to put the class down as authors.
2. Then review the book children explored in the previous mini-lesson, and talk about the sensory words. *Which sense do these words help describe?*
3. Show children the cover of the class big book. Then invite a child to take the hand drawing from the pocket chart and glue it to the cover.
4. Flip the book open, and generate a list of "touch" words with the class. You might let children glue the word cards from the previous mini-lesson to the paper, then write in new words children brainstorm. Encourage children to use the words in their writing.

Sample Touch Page

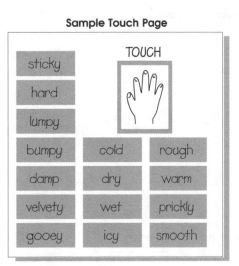

TOUCH

sticky · hard · lumpy · bumpy · cold · rough · damp · dry · warm · velvety · wet · prickly · gooey · icy · smooth

Emotive and Sensory Words:
Sense of Sight

(WRITING ELEMENT—INTERESTING/PRECISE WORDS)

Choose a piece of literature that will help students understand that authors carefully select special describing words to help the reader imagine a story. A great book with many such adjectives is *Rainbow Fish* by Marcus Pfister.

What to Do:

1. In your reading center, arrange the sensory big book, the pocket chart with the remaining sensory pictures, and your book choice. Then invite the class to the center.
2. Explain that today's reading selection will focus on words that describe how things look. *Which sense tells us this?* Ask a volunteer to come to the pocket chart, find the picture prompt (eye), and glue it to the cover of the big book.
3. Share the story with the class. Explain that you will not show them the pictures this time. Instead, you want them to close their eyes and listen to the words. *What pictures do the words paint in their minds?*

Sample Sight Page

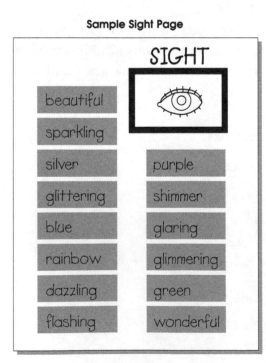

4. Proceed slowly. Stop at the end of each page, challenging children to tell you the sensory sight words. You might model a sentence to prompt their ideas, such as, "I could really see this fish in my mind because the author used words like . . ." Write children's words on a fresh big book page.
5. Read the list with the class. If time allows, you might let children dribble glitter glue over the letters to make them sparkle.

Pictures for Sensory Word Big Book

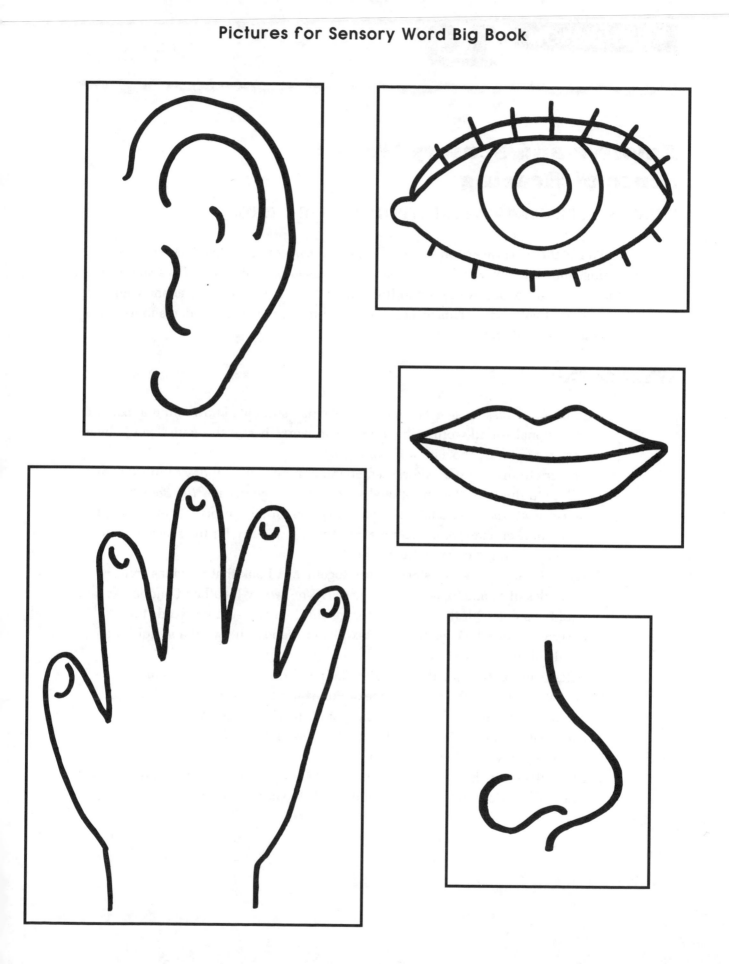

Emotive and Sensory Words:
Sense of Hearing

(WRITING ELEMENT—INTERESTING/PRECISE WORDS)

Words that describe sounds can fall into two categories—adjectives, such as *loud*, *blaring*, and *soft*; and words of *onomatopoeia*, or words that sound like a sound, like *crack*, *hiss*, and *boom*. Authors and illustrators have a tendency to use onomatopoeia in bold and lively ways. This makes it easy and fun for primary students to locate sensational sound words.

What to Do:

1. Prior to the lesson, select about ten books that students know and that contain sensational sound words. The mini-lesson works best if the sound words have been set apart by the author in some way.

2. Gather children to the reading center and announce that today's mini-lesson will help them fill the sensational sound word page in their *Big Book of Sensory Words*. Have students look at the remaining sensory picture prompts in the pocket chart. Ask a volunteer to find the picture for the sense of hearing and glue it to the cover of the big book.

3. Present the class with a story to read together. A book that provides great examples of onomatopoeia is *Froggy Gets Dressed* by Jonathan London. As you read the story with the class, encourage children to listen for words that describe a sound. When they do, ask them to repeat the word and hold their hands to their ears.

4. After reading the book through once, help children notice how sound words are set apart from the rest of the text. For example, in *Froggy Gets Dressed*, sound words are separated from the rest of the text with a dash and an exclamation point. You might let children place highlighter tape over the words so they stand out even more.

5. Show the class the other books you've selected for the mini-lesson. If time is available, choose examples of sound words to share with the class.

6. Then let students discover the sound words on their own. Buddy up students and give each a book to explore. Challenge them to find sensational sound words to write on the sound page of the class big book. Provide each pair with self-stick notes on which to write their words. Give children ample time to read and write.

7. Gather the children again, and invite them to share their sound words. Have them place their self-stick notes on the big book page. Later, rewrite the words in bold block letters. You might invite students to illustrate the words in fun, imaginative ways.

Sample Sound Page

Emotive and Sensory Words:
Sense of Hearing

(WRITING ELEMENT–INTERESTING/PRECISE WORDS)

To further stress that sensational sound words can add personality and style to children's writing, follow-up the previous mini-lesson with this center activity.

What to Do:

1. Set up the following materials in the center:
   - paints and brushes
   - small cups of water
   - sheets of white construction paper, cut in the same random, free-flowing shape (see example below)

Examples of Super-Sized, Sensational Sound Words

2. Tell children that you would like them to illustrate a super-sized, sensational sound word. Invite children to choose a fun sound word to illustrate. If necessary, assign sound words so none are duplicated. For younger children, write the sound words on paper ahead of time for them to color in.

3. Suggest that students first write the words in pencil, then paint and illustrate them. Instruct them to set the words aside to dry.

4. The next day, have children share their words, and then arrange them on a binder ring in the writing center for easy reference.

Emotive and Sensory Words: Senses of Taste and Smell

(WRITING ELEMENT–INTERESTING/PRECISE WORDS)

The senses of taste and smell are very much related, and often just one carefully chosen word can appeal to both senses. Encourage children to find words that make food sound "good enough to eat."

What to Do:

1. Some preparation is needed. Ahead of time, choose a book to share with the class that relies heavily on the senses of taste and smell. One book that works well is *The Sandwich That Max Made* by Marcia Vaughan. Go through the book and create cutouts for the foods featured. Place the food cutouts in a basket or bowl. On separate index cards, write the words that describe each food.

2. Then gather the class to the reading center. Display the pocket chart with the two remaining sensory prompt pictures. Challenge children to identify the senses, then let them glue the pictures to the cover of the sensory big book.

3. Present children with your basket or bowl of food cutouts, along with your book selection and the word cards with descriptive words. Pass out the food pictures to various students. Instruct children to listen closely as you read the story, and tell students with food pictures to stand up when they hear their foods.

4. Begin to read the story slowly, asking students to listen for the words that describe how a food tastes and smells. At the end of each page, invite the child with that food to find the word card that describes it. Let the child come to the pocket chart and slip in the food picture with the matching food word.

5. When all the foods have been described and the taste-and-smell words placed in the pocket chart, close the lesson with a taste-and-smell matching game. Collect all the words cards from the pocket chart. Mix up the cards. Then show a card to the class and ask them to read it. Challenge a student to match the card with the food it describes, then place it in the pocket chart next to the food for confirmation.

6. Finally, choose three students to glue the word cards to the smell-and-taste page of the sensory big book.

Tip! Make a second set of word cards, and let children enjoy the game again as a center activity.

Sample Smell and Taste Page

Emotive and Sensory Words: Emotive Words

(WRITING ELEMENT–INTERESTING/PRECISE WORDS)

Invite your students to explore how authors use a character's changing emotions to develop a story. Choose a piece of children's literature that provides examples of emotions. An outstanding example of a character full of emotions is Lilly in *Lilly's Purple Plastic Purse*.

What to Do:

1. Ahead of time, prepare a large sheet of chart or mural paper as shown below. Repeat this structure for each emotion children explore. Set up the chart in your reading center.

Lilly's Emotions	Lilly's Emotions	Lilly's Emotions
Beginning	Middle	End
_____ was (character name)	_____ was (character name)	_____ was (character name)
_____ because (emotive word)	_____ because (emotive word)	_____ because (emotive word)
_____ (event)	_____ (event)	_____ (event)
_____	_____	_____
_____	_____	_____
_____ was (character name)	_____ was (character name)	_____ was (character name)
_____ because (emotive word)	_____ because (emotive word)	_____ because (emotive word)
_____ (event)	_____ (event)	_____ (event)
_____	_____	_____
_____	_____	_____

2. Invite the class to the center. Hold up the reading selection and explain that for today's mini-lesson, children are going to look at how authors use a character's feelings and moods to develop a story.

3. Before you begin to read, brainstorm with children words that express how we feel. Record their responses separately from the chart. Mention that these words are *emotive words*. They help us understand story characters by describing their emotions.

4. Begin to read the book. Pause at a natural break or after the beginning of the story, and talk with children about the emotive words the author used to describe the character. *What events made the character feel this way?* Record

children's responses on the "Beginning" section of the chart. (For example, if your class is reading *Lilly's Purple Plastic Purse*, a good first break could be when Mr. Slinger has had enough.)

5. Continue reading the story. Pause after reading the "middle" section, and again talk about the character's feelings and the story events. (For Lilly, you might stop after Lilly admits she is sorry.) Again, record children's ideas on the chart, this time on the "Middle" section.

6. Finish reading the story, and once again ask students for the emotive words that describe how Lilly feels, along with the story events. Record their answers on the "End" part of the chart.

7. Talk with children about the emotive words they found. Encourage them to use these words to describe the feelings and moods of characters in their own stories.

Tip! Remember—one mini-lesson is often not enough to solidify a concept. Find other books with strong emotive words to explore with children in the same way. Other books and characters that work well include:

Sylvester in *Sylvester and the Magic Pebble* by William Steig

Jerome in *Jerome the Baby-Sitter* by Eileen Christelow

The children in *Miss Nelson Is Missing!* by James Marshall

Mama in *Mama, Do You Love Me?* by Barbara Joosse

Sample Beginning, Middle, and End Charts

Lilly's Emotions

Beginning

Lilly was happy because she loved school so much! (and Mr. Slinger, too!)

Lilly was especially happy because she had a new purple plastic purse filled with cool things.

Lilly was frustrated because she had to wait to show everyone.

Lilly's Emotions

Middle

Lilly was very sad because Mr. Slinger took her purse away!!

Lilly was angry and furious because she wanted her purse back!!

Lilly was feeling awful because Mr. Slinger gave back her purse with a nice note and some tasty snacks.

Lilly was REALLY sorry because she drew a mean picture and gave it to Mr. Slinger!!

Lilly's Emotions

End

Lilly was happy because she got to share her cool stuff and give a delicious snack to everyone!!

Lilly was so happy because it had been a BETTER day!!

MINI-LESSON **23**

Emotive and Sensory Words:
Emotive Words

(WRITING ELEMENT—INTERESTING/PRECISE WORDS)

Another wonderful way to explore moods and feelings is to share the book *Today I Feel Silly and Other Moods That Make My Day*, by Jamie Lee Curtis.

What to Do:

1. Ahead of time, create a chart on a long sheet of mural or butcher paper. List these emotions in separate columns across the top: *silly, angry, excited, cranky, happy,* and *sad.* Hang the chart in your reading center. (See sample chart below.) Reproduce and cut apart the faces on page 75.

Today I Feel...

silly	angry	excited	cranky	happy	sad
• put rouge on the cat	• face is all pinched and red ear to ear	• going to sell cookies and lemonade at school	• has diarrhea	• walking on air	• frown on her face
• put gloves on her feet	• friends left her out	• starting a club to clean up the park	• broke her new kite	• learned how to knit	• had a really big fight with best friend
• ate noodles for breakfast	• wants to shout	• has a big crush on teacher	• mom dyed her hair orange	• learned how to French-braid hair	• friend said that she tattled (she did)
• ate pancakes at night			• dad shaved his beard	• did first solo in hip-hop	
			• tooth came in crooked	• full of pizzazz	
			• family is weird		

2. Gather the class to the center, and explain that today's mini-lesson will once again focus on character emotions and the events that affect those emotions. Hold up the book *Today I Feel Silly and Other Moods That Make My Day*, and show students the mood wheel in the back. Point out that you have written the emotions from the wheel on the chart paper.

3. Begin to read the story with the class. Pause after each emotion and discuss it. Ask a volunteer to show on the mood wheel what a person might look like when feeling this mood or emotion.

4. Then talk about the events that either *caused* the character to feel this way or what the character did *because* she felt this way. Record the story events in the proper column on the chart. Also let a volunteer glue the face picture for that emotion next to the emotion word at the top of the column.

5. Repeat the procedure for the other emotions in the story.

6. After reading, review the emotions with the class.

7. Then encourage children to choose one mood or emotion about which to create a story character. Instruct them to draw a picture of their character doing something because of the mood the character is in.

8. Conclude by asking children to write a brief description for their character pictures that explains how the character feels and what the character is doing. Guide children's writing by suggesting that they start their descriptions with *Today (story character) feels (emotive word).* Invite children to share their characters and descriptions with classmates.

silly

happy

angry

cranky

sad

excited

"Vigorous" Verbs

(WRITING ELEMENT–INTERESTING/PRECISE WORDS)

Your students' writing can become even more enhanced when they begin including "vigorous" verbs. In her book *Kites Sail High*, Ruth Heller describes a verb as "the most superb of any word you've ever heard," and claims that "a vigorous verb is super superb." When children begin to experiment with verbs that precisely describe actions, you will notice a real improvement in the quality of their writing.

What to Do:

1. Ahead of time, choose a story that children already know that contains a variety of "vigorous" verbs. On sentence strips, write the character's name who acts out the verb, along with the "vigorous" verb. Then cut the two words—character name and verb—apart.

2. Invite children to the reading center. If possible, introduce them to "vigorous" verbs by sharing selected pages from *Kites Sail High*. Explain that the author has written an entire book about verbs, or action words. As you read the book, allow children to enjoy the language and illustrations. Be sure to point out that the verbs are the words printed in bold letters.

3. Then read the story you selected ahead of time. Go through the story, page by page, stopping to encourage children to find the verbs that describe what the character is doing. As they do so, invite children to come to the pocket chart and place the character name (noun) and the action word (verb) side by side in the pocket chart. (The pocket chart on page 77 is an example from *Froggy Gets Dressed*.)

4. After reading the book and finding and recording the "vigorous" verbs, encourage students to choose a verb to illustrate. Suggest that they draw a picture of the book character engaged in the action the verb describes. Tell them to also write the short noun/verb sentence below their pictures. Large index cards work well for this activity.

5. While children work, set up a chart on a sheet of mural or butcher paper, as shown on page 78. As students finish their drawings and sentences, invite them to glue the index cards to the paper below the title of the book they read.

6. Repeat this mini-lesson over the next several days, each time exploring a new book for "vigorous" verbs. Each time, let children select verbs to illustrate and write about to add to the chart.

Sample Pocket Chart Reinforcing Noun-Verb Pattern

Verb = Action (doing)			
Froggy	buttoned	Tucker	bounded
Froggy	snapped	Tucker	crashed
Froggy	tugged	Tucker	jumped
Froggy	pulled	Tucker	raced
Froggy	tied	Tucker	flew
Froggy	flopped	Tucker	zigzagged
		Tucker	slipped
		Tucker	knocked
		Tucker	came running

Chart for "Vigorous" Verbs (Mini-Lesson 24)

Some Vigorous Actions of Our Favorite Characters

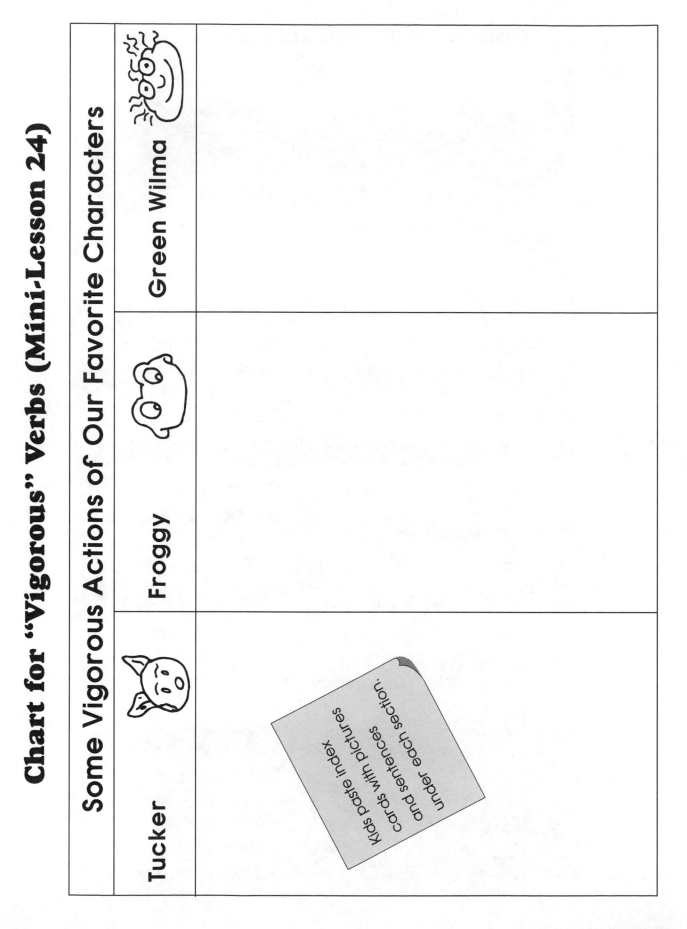

Tucker	Froggy	Green Wilma

Kids paste index cards with pictures and sentences under each section.

"Vigorous" Verbs

(WRITING ELEMENT-INTERESTING/PRECISE WORDS)

To further engage children in exploring "vigorous" verbs, encourage them to play a round of "Vigorous" Verbs Charades.

What to Do:

1. Ahead of time, choose a book with verbs you would like to use for the mini-lesson. The mini-lesson works best if the book is one for which verbs have already been recorded and discussed in Mini-Lesson 24. Create a headband for the main character associated with the verbs.

2. Then gather children to the reading center. Display the pocket chart or butcher-paper chart with the "vigorous" verbs children discovered from that story. Choose a volunteer to stand before the group, and place the character headband on the child's head.

3. Whisper a "vigorous" verb from the chart to the child, and instruct the child to act out that verb. Challenge the rest of the class to guess the verb.

4. When the verb has been correctly identified, remove it from the pocket chart. Repeat with another child and another verb. Continue until all the verbs have been acted out.

"Vigorous" Verbs

(WRITING ELEMENT–INTERESTING/PRECISE WORDS)

To further sharpen children's awareness of "vigorous" verbs, encourage them to create a class book of "vigorous" verbs with this mini-lesson.

What to Do:

1. Ahead of time, choose a book or two that you have yet to search for "vigorous" verbs. Wonderful selections include *In the Tall, Tall Grass* and *In the Small, Small Pond* by Denise Fleming.

2. With little introduction, slowly begin to read the book. Challenge children to figure out why you have chosen this book as a mini-lesson for writing. Hopefully, children will notice that each page is filled with "vigorous" verbs.

3. Once they do, go back to the beginning and begin to read again. This time, stop after each page, and ask children to tell you what the character in the story is *doing*. Repeat children's responses to confirm their answers. (For example, "Yes! The beetles *skitter*.")

4. After reading, invite children to contribute to a class book of verbs. Set up art tables with watercolors and same-sized art paper. Instruct children to paint a scene that shows a lot of action, preferably related to the book you read. Set aside the pictures to dry.

5. Have children tape writing paper to the bottom of each drawing, then write sentences with "vigorous" verbs to describe the actions.

6. Let children share their work, then bind the pages together into a class book to keep in your reading center for reference.

Rain Forest

The rain forest is very colorful. The scarlet macaw is golden yellow and tomato red. The deep green leaves decorate the gigantic trees. Sunshine yellow, hot pink, and ocean blue lay on the bodies of the poisonous frog. The fluttering butterfly is filled with lots of breathtaking colors. All the bright colors in the rain forest blind me.

Tip! This mini-lesson could be spread out over several days. Be flexible and creative with the time young writers need. Extensions like this one that involve various learning modalities help foster concept development.

Home-Run Sentences

(WRITING ELEMENT–SENTENCE BUILDING AND
PARAGRAPH ORGANIZING)

Beginning writers often fall into the trap of writing very simple sentences. They labor over spelling, punctuation, and grammar, often telling their ideas in as few words as possible. Unknowingly, they are writing uninteresting and sometimes incomplete sentences. Now that students have come up with lists of exciting words, encourage them to include the words in "home-run" sentences.

What to Do:

1. Prior to the mini-lesson, you will need to find an example of a child's writing to share with the class. Choose the work of a child who has rather good penmanship and somewhat accurate spelling. You will need to find an example of a simple sentence that can be turned into a home-run sentence.
2. Ask the child for permission to use the story for a class lesson. Explain that the story will help you teach a very important writing lesson to the class. (This is great to booster self-esteem!)
3. Then reproduce the child's writing on a transparency for the overhead.
4. Gather the class to the reading center and display the transparency. Invite the student author to come to the overhead and share the story.
5. After the reading, have the class ask questions about the story. Most likely, the author will easily be able to answer the questions. Speculate how the child's answers could have been included in the sentences, providing the reader with more information.

Home-Run Sentences

(WRITING ELEMENT—SENTENCE BUILDING AND
PARAGRAPH ORGANIZING)

Continue to study a student author's sentences, building them into home-run winners.

What to Do:

1. Ahead of time, reproduce the Home-Run Sentence sheet on page 83 onto a transparency.
2. Then review the story the class heard the previous day that was written by their classmate. Choose one simple sentence from the story, and write it on the first-base line of the transparency.
3. Display the baseball diamond on the transparency, and encourage children to talk about the game of baseball. *What is the significance of a home run? What does a player do who hits a home run?* (The player runs around the bases and scores a run.)

4. Then explain that children can turn simple, first-base sentences into home-run, game-winning sentences by adding details. Ask children to read the first-base sentence. *Would the rest of the class like to know more?* Have them question the author, prompting him or her to add details. Each time they do, write the revised sentence on the next line around the base. Record any question words inside the baseball diamond.
5. Conclude by letting students read the super home-run sentence and cheer for the batter-writer. (See example at left.)

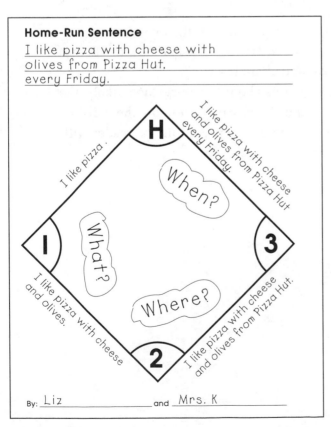

Home-Run Sentence

I like pizza with cheese with
olives from Pizza Hut,
every Friday.

H

I like pizza.

I like pizza with cheese
and olives from Pizza Hut
every Friday.

When?

What?

Where?

I
I like pizza
and olives.

1
I like pizza with cheese
and olives.

2
I like pizza with cheese
and olives from Pizza Hut.

3

By: Liz   and Mrs. K

Home-Run Sentence

_____

_____

_____

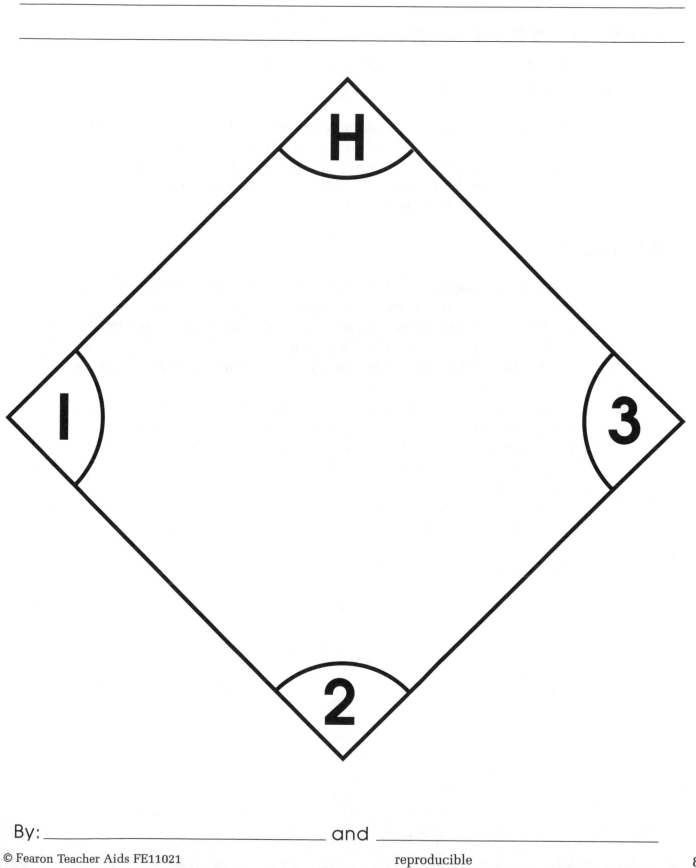

By: _____ and _____

reproducible

Sentence Stretching

(WRITING ELEMENT–SENTENCE BUILDING AND
PARAGRAPH ORGANIZING)

Just because you model a procedure once does not mean that all children will immediately understand it. Improving writing takes time. You can incorporate the home-run idea into other curriculum areas, including science and social studies. This will further ingrain the lesson children are trying to learn. For an extra mini-lesson, explore *The Fish Book* on pages 85–87.

What to Do:

1. Reproduce the pages of *The Fish Book*. Give a copy to each child. Instruct students to cut the pages apart, then staple them together in order.

2. Then gather children to your reading center, and invite them to take turns reading pages from the story. Provide no introduction. Challenge children to figure out the pattern of the sentences. Confirm that the sentences are built on each other until they become home runs.

3. Carefully reread each page with the group, asking children to supply a question word that was answered by the additional sentence information.

4. Encourage the class to write other stories based on the format of *The Fish Book*. Some first-base sentences might be:
   - The mouse ran fast.
   - The boy looked out his window.
   - Grandma was cooking.
   - We went to the zoo.
   - The Native American girl was working.

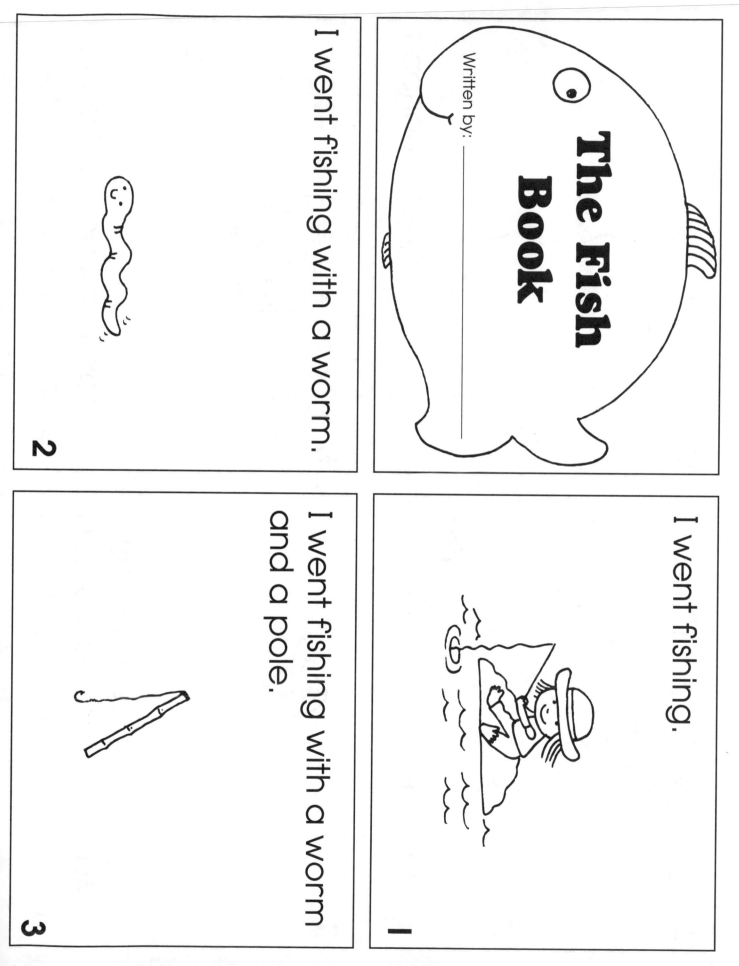

I went fishing with a worm.

2

The Fish Book

Written by: _____

I went fishing.

1

I went fishing with a worm and a pole.

3

reproducible

I went fishing with a worm and a pole on Saturday.

4

I went fishing with a worm and a pole on Saturday with my friend.

5

I caught a fish.

6

I caught a fish that was big.

7

reproducible

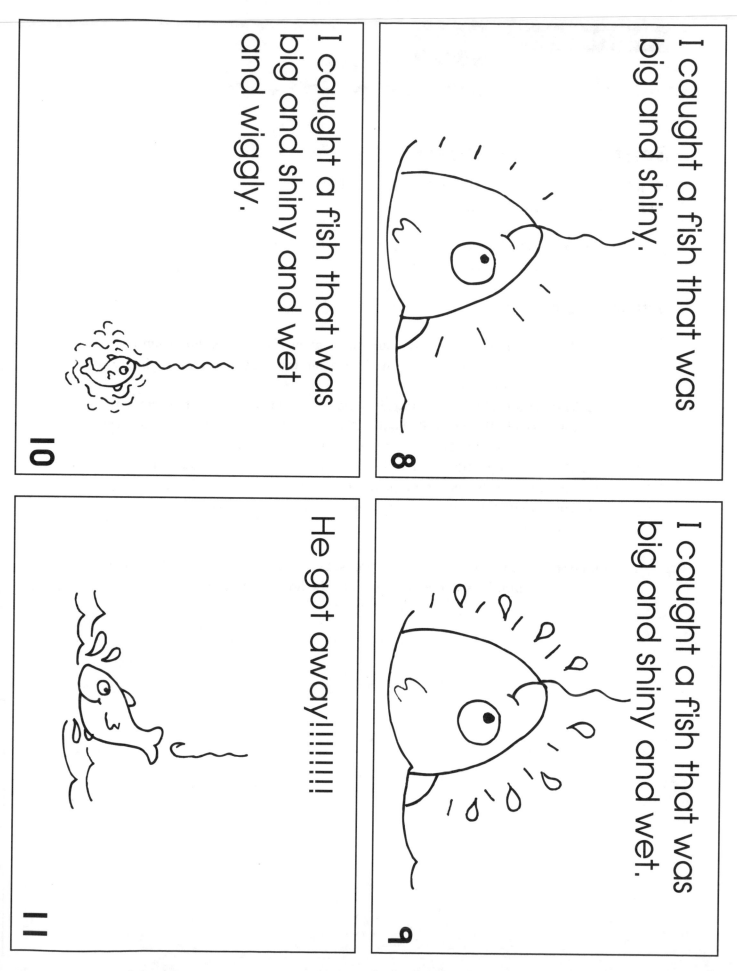

8

I caught a fish that was big and shiny.

10

I caught a fish that was big and shiny and wet and wiggly.

9

I caught a fish that was big and shiny and wet.

11

He got away!!!!!!!!

reproducible

Sentence Stretching

(WRITING ELEMENT–SENTENCE BUILDING AND
PARAGRAPH ORGANIZING)

With this mini-lesson, challenge children to find other home-run sentences in books you have in class.

What to Do:

1. Review with children why home-run sentences are super. For example, they give lots of details, answer questions about the story, and they are interesting and fun to read.
2. Then arrange the class into pairs, and challenge children to find home-run sentences in their favorite books. Give each pair some self-stick notes with which to mark the book pages that have home-run sentences.
3. Set aside ample time for children to explore the literature, reading the pages for home-run sentences and marking each page with a self-stick note.
4. Then invite the pairs to share their sentences, explaining why they are home runs.

 Tip! For added fun, bring in baseball props. Let partners wear baseball hats and swing plastic mini-bats as one partner reads the home-run sentence.

Sentence Stretching

(WRITING ELEMENT–SENTENCE BUILDING AND
PARAGRAPH ORGANIZING)

This step in sentence stretching is to model how to effectively question a classmate during peer conferencing. Hold a mini-lesson on peer conferencing to talk about, critique, and discuss each other's home-run sentences.

What to Do:

1. Ahead of time, reproduce enough copies of the Revision Chart on page 90 for your class.
2. Pass out the Revision Chart, then invite two students to the front of the class. Encourage them to model for their classmates how to effectively conference with each other. Be sure they focus on questioning and that the questioning leads to revision. Also make sure they use the Revision Chart.
3. Then assign children to partners to participate in peer conferences. Suggest that as they are asked questions by their classmates, they write the answers on self-stick notes to apply to those pages of their writing. This way, valuable feedback will not be lost or forgotten.
4. When peer conferencing is completed, let students return to their desks to revise their writing, referring to the feedback provided by their peers.

Tip! For younger children, you might just have them check Steps 1 and 2 on the Revision Chart, rather than write out the questions and details.

Revision Chart

Title of my story:

_____

_____

☐ **1.** My friend asked me questions about my story. Here are my friend's questions:

_____

_____

_____

_____

☐ **2.** I added more details to my story. Here are the details I added:

_____

_____

_____

_____

My Name: _____

My Friend's Name: _____

reproducible

Composing Sentences with Different Beginnings

(WRITING ELEMENT–SENTENCE BUILDING AND
PARAGRAPH ORGANIZING)

Because children are often so involved in relaying the message of their writing, they may not think about word choice and flow. This becomes evident when sentences all begin with the same word. The following mini-lesson will help children reconstruct such sentences.

What to Do:

1. Ahead of time, choose a piece of writing that has been composed by your class in an interactive writing session. The piece should have sentences with the same beginning word. Transfer the writing to chart paper to display in your reading center. You could also use the example below:

> **Frogs**
> Frogs live in ponds.
> Frogs lay small eggs in the water.
> Frogs have strong back legs.
> Frogs can jump far!

2. Gather children to the reading center, and invite them to read the sentences along with you.
3. Ask volunteers to place a piece of highlighting tape over the first word in each sentence. Invite another student to read each highlighted word. *What do children notice?*
4. Hopefully, children will see that all the beginning words are the same. Capitalize on this discovery by guiding children to rewrite the sentences so they have different beginnings. Brainstorm a list of words that could replace *frogs*. You might let children look through other texts for ideas. Model flipping through the books and thinking out loud which words could replace *frogs* in their sentences. List children's ideas. Some possibilities include:

they	**cold-blooded creatures**
slippery little fellows	**green jumping machines**
amphibians	

5. Have children choose which words they'd like to use in the sentences on the chart, and write them on sentence strips. Let children tape the new words over the repeated beginning words. Then invite students to read the new sentences along with you.

> **Frogs**
> Frogs live in ponds.
> These amphibians lay small eggs in the water.
> They have strong back legs.
> These green jumping machines can jump far!

6. Talk with children about how the sentences sound better together. Reaffirm the lesson by letting children read other pieces the class has written together to find and replace repeated beginning words.

Composing Sentences with Different Beginnings

(WRITING ELEMENT–SENTENCE BUILDING AND
PARAGRAPH ORGANIZING)

Now that children have had practice finding and replacing repeated beginning words, let them improve their own writing by following the same procedure.

What to Do:

1. Tell children to choose a piece of their own writing that has many sentences with the same beginning words that they would like to improve.
2. Working with a highlighter, have children highlight each beginning word that is the same.
3. On a separate sheet of paper, ask students to think about and write down words that could be used instead of the repeated words. If necessary, provide time for children to flip through other texts for ideas.
4. Instruct children to rewrite their sentences with the new beginning words.
5. Conference with students to check their work. At this time, find examples of children's writing that aptly shows "before" and "after" sentences—*before* sentences with repeated beginning words and *after* sentences that have been improved. With the author's permission, write the sentences on transparencies or chart paper.
6. Share the sentences with the class. Read each set, leading children to hear that the improved sentences flow and read more smoothly.

Paragraph Writing

(WRITING ELEMENT–SENTENCE BUILDING AND
PARAGRAPH ORGANIZING)

Next to sentences, paragraphs are probably the most essential components of
writing. Most beginning writers may not realize that paragraphs are put together in
specific ways. Once you break it down for them, they'll be composing clear,
organized paragraphs in no time. The book *Literature and Cooperative Learning* by
Nancy Whisler presents lessons for upper-grade students on writing paragraphs.
The following mini-lessons contain adaptations of her work, made more appropriate
for primary writers.

What to Do:

1. Ahead of time, prepare five paper strips in different colors of construction
   paper. You will need:
   - ✔ 1 Red Strip   Paragraph Title
   - ✔ 1 White Strip with Black Arrow Paragraph Indent
   - ✔ 1 Yellow Strip   Main Idea Sentence
   - ✔ 3 Green Strips   Detail Sentences
   - ✔ 1 Yellow Strip   Wrap-Around/Concluding Sentence

2. You will also need to prepare label cards and picture cues to place in the
   pocket chart. Patterns for these labels and pictures are provided on pages
   96–99.

3. Finally, copy a paragraph onto sentence strips for students to place in the
   appropriate place on the pocket chart. The paragraph below has been
   provided for your convenience, but feel free to use any paragraph, especially
   one related to a topic you are currently studying. Be sure the sentence strips
   are the same size as the row of the pocket chart. Tape the strips in order to
   the chalkboard for children to see, along with the labels, colored strips, and
   picture cues for the pocket chart.

Frogs

Frogs are interesting amphibians. When they swallow, they blink. Frogs have
long sticky tongues for catching flies. They have webbed feet so they can swim.
Frogs are the most interesting creatures I have ever written about.

4. Gather children to the reading center. Explain that today's mini-lesson will help them learn about the five important parts of a paragraph.

5. Speculate with children what the first part of the paragraph might be. Have them look at the sentence strips for guidance. When someone suggests "the title," invite children to remove the title label, picture cues, and colored strip from the chalkboard and place it in the pocket chart. As they do so, explain that the title is really the *topic*, or main idea, of the paragraph. That's why the title on the chart is indicated by the picture cue of a lightbulb (for *idea*).

6. Continue this way for the other paragraph components. Discussion for each could be as follows:

● *Paragraph Indent:* A paragraph must always begin by moving the first line over to the right. This lets the reader know that a new paragraph has begun. The arrow should help them remember to move the first line to the right, or *indent* it. Let children place the arrow icons in the pocket chart.

● *Main Idea Sentence:* The first sentence of the paragraph lets the reader know what the writer is about to tell them. Have students find the Main Idea Sentence icon, label, and colored strip to place next to the arrow on the pocket chart.

● *Detail Sentences:* The next thing a good writer needs when building a paragraph are sentences that help support, or hold up, the main idea sentence. This is done by writing details that describe or prove the main idea. Ask volunteers to place the green strips and corresponding labels and picture cues in the pocket chart.

● *Wrap-Around Sentence:* The last part of a paragraph is the last sentence. Have students study the picture cue, noticing how the arrow wraps around and points back up to the main idea sentence. This sentence usually sums up what the first sentence explained. Have students place the yellow strip, label, and picture cue in the pocket chart.

7. Stand back and review with children the complete paragraph components.

8. Culminate by challenging children to place the sentence strips for the actual paragraph with the correct colored strips in the pocket chart.

 Tip! The pocket-chart paragraph makes a great center activity!

Pocket Chart Paragraph

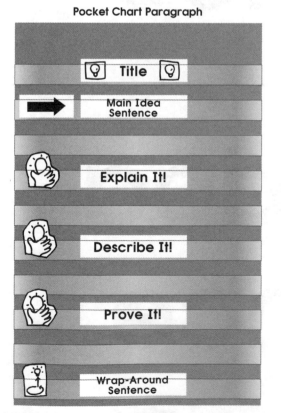

Title

Wrap-Around Sentence

Main Idea Sentence

reproducible

Describe It!

Explain It!

Prove It!

reproducible

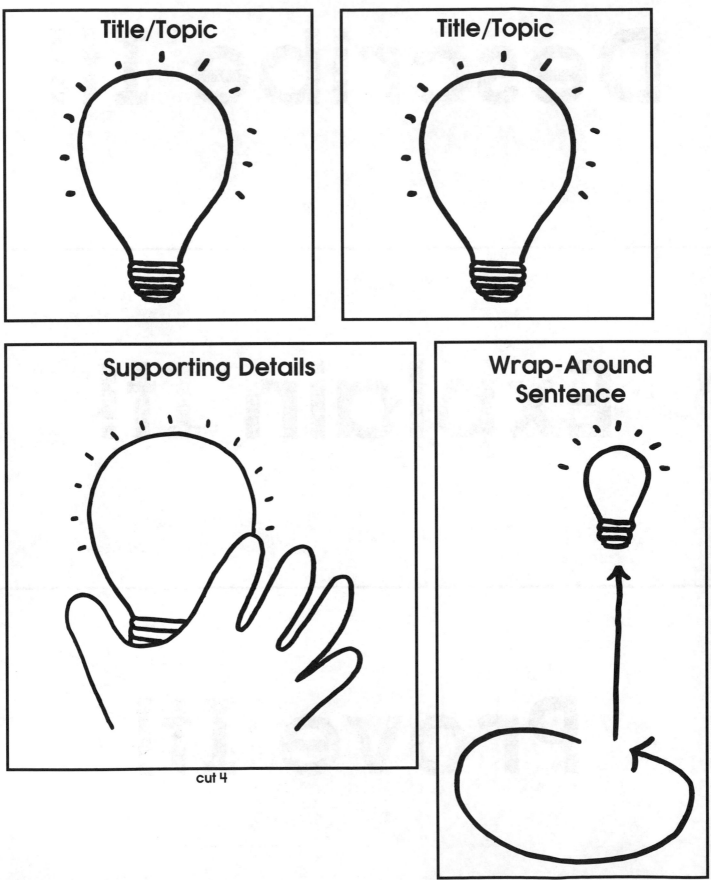

Title/Topic

Title/Topic

Supporting Details

cut 4

Wrap-Around Sentence

cut 1

Paragraph Indent Card

reproducible

Paragraph Writing

(WRITING ELEMENT—SENTENCE BUILDING AND
PARAGRAPH ORGANIZING)

Provide further practice for finding and understanding the parts of a paragraph with this mini-lesson.

What to Do:

1. Ahead of time, prepare several paragraphs for children to examine. You might compose these paragraphs yourself, or reproduce those on page 101. Make enough copies so each child has his or her own set. You will also need to reproduce the paragraphs on transparencies for the overhead.

2. Give each child copies of the paragraphs. Ask children to bring out their crayons, colored pencils, or markers. Have each child hold up the color representing each paragraph part (red—title; black—indent; yellow— main idea sentence and wrap-around sentence; green—detail sentences).

3. Instruct children to find each part of the paragraph as indicated in the pocket chart from the previous mini-lesson, and underline it with the matching color. Model the activity on the overhead, inviting students to assist you. As each part is found, tell students to underline the parts on their paragraphs, as well.

4. Repeat the process over the next few days to strengthen the skill. Let children take home the sheets to complete as homework.

My Birthday

My birthday is the best day of all. We always have a party. All my friends come over and bring gifts. We have cake, ice cream, games, and prizes. I wish every day could be my birthday!

Owls

Owls are nocturnal animals. You can hear them hooting at night. In the dark they use their sharp eyes to catch food. They sleep during the day and hunt at night. Owls are birds of the night.

reproducible

MINI-LESSON 36

Paragraph Writing

(WRITING ELEMENT–LAYOUT/FLOW)

Students sometimes have trouble writing good wrap-around sentences. The mini-lesson below focuses on this important paragraph component.

What to Do:

1. Compose a paragraph without a wrap-around sentence for children to examine. The paragraphs on page 103 do not have wrap-around sentences. Write or reproduce these paragraphs on a transparency for the overhead.
2. Read a paragraph with the class. Invite students to come to the overhead and highlight the various parts of the paragraph. Hopefully, children will realize that the wrap-around sentence is missing.
3. Encourage children to offer ideas for wrap-around sentences. Let children confer, then record and discuss their ideas. Decide which is the most appropriate, supported by reasons.
4. Then write the wrap-around sentence at the end of the paragraph. Invite children to read the final paragraph with you. Conclude by letting a student underline the wrap-around sentence with the appropriate color.
5. Repeat with the second paragraph.

The Beach
Going to the beach is so much fun. You can swim, surf, or just lay in the sun. Some people like to build sand castles. I like eating all the picnic foods.

The Native Americans of the Plains
The Native Americans of the Plains used the things around them to make whatever they needed. The skins of animals became their clothes, shoes, and even part of their homes. They wove grasses into baskets and bowls. Weapons were made from rocks, stones, and wood.

Paragraph Writing

(WRITING ELEMENT–LAYOUT/FLOW)

The best way, of course, to check if children have adequately grasped how a paragraph is composed is to invite children to write paragraphs of their own. Guide children with this mini-lesson.

What to Do:

Sample Paragraph Form

My Topic: How Penguins Move

➡ My topic sentence: Penguins move in
many different ways.

My supporting details:
#1 Penguins swim easily in the water using their
strong flippers and webbed feet.

#2 When they want to get out of the water,
they dive deeply and then torpedo right out,
landing on the ice.

#3 Walking on land with webbed feet causes
penguins to waddle back and forth.

#4 When waddling becomes too difficult,
penguins plop down on their bellies and
toboggan across the ice.

My wrap-around sentence:
Penguins have learned how to move easily on
land and in water.

1. Ahead of time, reproduce the form on page 105 so each child has one. Also display your pocket chart with the paragraph components.
2. Pass out the form, and have children compare the information on the form with the information on the pocket chart. What do they think this form guides them to do? Children should conclude that the form will help them write a paragraph.
3. Encourage children to do so. Provide them with a theme, preferably one you and your class are currently investigating. For example, if you are studying ocean animals, children could choose an ocean animal to write about. Confer with students briefly to approve their topics.
4. Then instruct students to write sentences for their paragraphs on their forms. An example of a completed form is provided, as well as samples of actual paragraphs written by second-grade students.

Sample Paragraphs

Whales by Jessie

Whales are graceful.
They jump out of the water.
They're beautiful when they
swim. Their tails slap the water.
A whale's blowhole squirts out
water. I enjoy watching the
whale's graceful moves.

Dolphins by Brittany

Dolphins are very nice!
They save people's lives.
The dolphins let some people
touch them. Dolphins let people
ride on them. Sometimes dolphins
tell people if they have a hole
in their boat. I wish I had a
dolphin because they are so kind!

Name _____

💡 My Topic: _____

➡ My topic sentence: _____

_____

_____

_____

My supporting details:

#1 _____

_____

_____

#2 _____

_____

_____

#3 _____

_____

_____

#4 _____

_____

_____

My wrap-around sentence: _____

_____

_____

Layout/Flow

Young authors often have wonderful story ideas and appealing characters. However, putting it all together can be a mystery. They need help in relaying their story in a clear, organized manner. Teachers need to provide the scaffolding for students to produce writing that is sequential and well developed. In order to assist students with this difficult task, you might break down layout/flow into the following specific elements:

SEQUENCING

Beginning, Middle, End
Order Words
Connecting Words

STORY BUILDING

Structures and Matrixes
(How Text Works)

LEADS

Sequencing

Many times, young authors fail to tell the whole story. They may have a detailed beginning and a middle that holds the reader's attention, but their ending comes up short. Or, they know how the story begins and ends, but they don't know how to build the story in between. The following mini-lessons will provide students with practice in looking at the whole story and in the use of order and connecting words to show sequence.

Sequencing: Somebody/Wanted/But/So

(WRITING ELEMENT–LAYOUT/FLOW)

Before children can begin to write their own stories with well-developed beginnings, middles, and ends, they need practice analyzing stories they know. Dr. Barbara Schmidt created a framework that helps primary students tell the "whole story." This structure, known as "Somebody/Wanted/But/So," guides children to focus on events at the beginning, middle, and end of a story. The following mini-lesson lets students practice with this structure, based on a book you read together.

What to Do:

1. Prior to the lesson, prepare a large sheet of chart paper. Divide the paper into four squares. Write one word—*Somebody, Wanted, But, So*—at the top of each square in large, bold letters. Then choose a well-known and well-loved story to model. The example on this page is based on *Mrs. Wishy-Washy* by Joy Cowley.

Sample Chart for *Mrs. Wishy-Washy*

2. Gather the class to the reading center. Display the book and the chart. Explain that for today's writing lesson, they will look at a simple way to tell the *whole story*. Point to the chart and mention that these four words can help them do this. Then read the story.

3. Afterward, challenge children to help you complete the chart. Who was the *somebody* in the story? What did the somebody *want? But* what happened instead? *So,* what finally happened at the end? For each word, draw a picture to reflect the story plot.

4. Review the chart, guiding children to realize that with these four words, they've retold the *whole story.*

Sequencing: Somebody/Wanted/But/So

(WRITING ELEMENT–LAYOUT/FLOW)

As always, the more practice children have, the better able they are to grasp a concept. For further practice with "Somebody/Wanted/But/So," guide children through this mini-lesson.

What to Do:

1. Choose another favorite book to read with the class. Make copies of the chart on page 109, as well as a transparency for the overhead.

2. Share the book with the class, then pass out the chart. Explain that you want children to draw along with you as they explore the "Somebody/Wanted/But/So" of the story.

3. Follow the same procedure as outlined in Mini-Lesson 38. Draw the pictures on your overhead transparency as children draw on their own papers. Be sure to reinforce the words *somebody, wanted, but,* and *so,* and allow time for meaningful discussion.

4. When complete, cut apart your transparency, separating each quadrant. Mix up the squares. Challenge volunteers to come to the overhead and retell the story while placing the pieces in order.

5. Then give each child a small plastic baggie. Tell students to cut apart their own papers and place the pieces in the bags to take home. Explain that you would like them to share the story with their families, telling it in correct sequence as they arrange the pieces in story order. Instruct children to have a parent or other family member sign the back of one square so you can check for completion.

"Somebody/Wanted/But/So" Chart

Somebody

Wanted

But

So

Adapted from Dr. Barbara Schmidt

Sequencing: Somebody/Wanted/But/So— Writing Application

(WRITING ELEMENT–LAYOUT/FLOW)

After much guided practice in analyzing stories using "Somebody/Wanted/But/So," students will be ready to write stories of their own. The stories might be very simple at first. The goal is to move children through the story sequentially. As children become more comfortable with the format, they can add other "Sos" and "Buts" to make their stories more complex.

What to Do:

1. Prior to the lesson, prepare chart paper with the "Somebody/Wanted/But/So" format.

2. Gather children to the center and present the chart (page 109). Explain that as a group, they are going to write a story, using these words to guide them. Invite children to join you in reading the key words.

3. Point to the word *somebody*. Brainstorm ideas for who the "somebody" of their story could be. You might list children's ideas on a separate sheet, then take a class vote. Draw and label the story character in the "Somebody" box. (For example, "Little Bear.")

4. Then speculate with children what Little Bear might want to do. Again, you could list ideas, then ask children to vote on their favorite. ("Great! Little Bear wants a birthday party!") Draw and write about the idea in the "Wanted" box.

5. Point to the next word, *but*. Consider with children what could happen to prevent Little Bear's party. Flesh out ideas, and write and illustrate the final choice in the "But" box.

6. Finally, encourage children to think about how the story will end. How does the "but" problem get fixed? How is Little Bear able to have his party? Write and draw children's idea in the "So" box.

7. Close the lesson by having children join you in reading the story in order.

Tip! Be sure to guide your students through this procedure at least one more time before you send them off to write their own stories. The example on page 111 is from an actual children's story written using the "Somebody/Wanted/But/So" structure.

Sample Student Chart

Somebody	Wanted
Scamper Penguin	to play with Peter

But	So
He can't because he is having a dinner.	He finished his food and played with Peter.

Sample Student Story

Scamper Penguin

Written and Illustrated by Daniela

Time for dinner Scamper.

I'm Peter.

Scamper wanted to play with Peter.

But he can't because he is haveing dinner.

I'm going out.

So he finished his food and played with Peter.

Sequencing: Order Words—The Day

(WRITING ELEMENT–LAYOUT/FLOW)

Order words help move a reader along with the flow of a story. Students probably already use order words in their daily language without realizing it. And basically, it is the same approach when writing. This activity is a fun and easy way to practice with order words as students talk about their day.

What to Do:

1. Ahead of time, write the words *First, Next, Then,* and *Last* on chart paper, as shown on page 113. You might laminate the chart to use again.
2. At the end of the school day, gather children around the chart. Explain that this chart helps them organize what they did that day. Invite a volunteer to read the words, and mention that they are *order words*. They tell us the order in which things happened.
3. Then ask children what was the first thing they did that day. Record their responses in the "first" section. Move from section to section, discussing and recording children's ideas.
4. When complete, reread the chart with the class, pointing out how easily they organized the day using order words.

Tip! It is not necessary to do the activity every day. You might choose to do it on special days, like field trips and class parties.

What Happened Today?

First

We bought candy and cupcakes for the Halloween party.

Next

We did our calendar and took a spelling test.

Then

We went outside and played games. We bobbed for apples and played pin the tail on the cat.

Last

We ate our food!

Sequencing: Order Words—Cooking

(WRITING ELEMENT–LAYOUT/FLOW)

Cooking in the classroom places order words in an authentic setting. If time and facilities allow, plan a cooking activity that helps children practice using *first, then, next,* and *last*. Be sure to write the recipe on chart paper, stressing the order words.

What to Do:

1. Ahead of time, choose a simple recipe to make with the class. The book *Book Cooks* by Janet Bruno has excellent recipes for young cooks. Rewrite the recipe in four steps so it coincides with the words *first, then, next,* and *last.* Add illustrations to the recipe, too. Finally, write each word—*first, then, next,* and *last*—on a craft stick.

2. Divide the class into four cooking teams. Place your labeled craft sticks in a cup, and invite a member from each group to choose one. Have each child read the word and explain when it will be his or her turn to complete the recipe.

3. Read through the recipe with the entire class, then invite each group—*first, then, next,* and *last*—to the cooking center at the appropriate time to assist. Depending on the age of your students, you might enlist the aid of a parent volunteer or older student.

Sample Recipe Chart for *First*, *Then*, *Next*, and *Last*

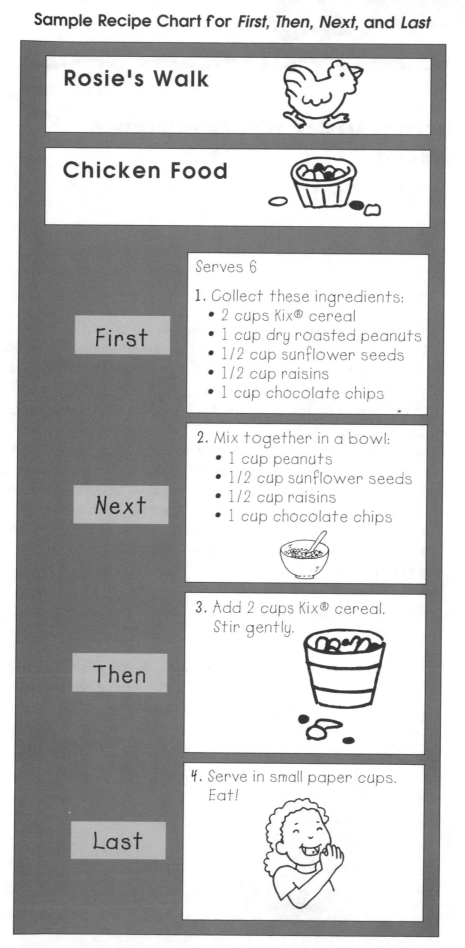

Rosie's Walk

Chicken Food

First

Serves 6

1. Collect these ingredients:
   • 2 cups Kix® cereal
   • 1 cup dry roasted peanuts
   • 1/2 cup sunflower seeds
   • 1/2 cup raisins
   • 1 cup chocolate chips

Next

2. Mix together in a bowl:
   • 1 cup peanuts
   • 1/2 cup sunflower seeds
   • 1/2 cup raisins
   • 1 cup chocolate chips

Then

3. Add 2 cups Kix® cereal. Stir gently.

Last

4. Serve in small paper cups. Eat!

Sequencing: Order Words—Science Experiment

(WRITING ELEMENT–LAYOUT/FLOW)

Science is another area in which following a sequence is important. Help children organize a science experiment with order words.

What to Do:

1. Set up this mini-lesson to take place during science time. Present children with a science experiment tied in to your current science theme. Explain that they are going to do this experiment in steps—*first, then, next,* and *last.* Challenge children to tell you why these words sound familiar, and confirm that they are exploring the use of these words in their writing to help organize stories.

2. Then review the experiment with the class, using the order words. As children watch and read along with you, write the steps of the experiment, prefaced by the order words. For example, maybe your class has been studying plants and they are about to plant their own. Model phrases such as:
   - *"First,* we will get the seeds and some soil."
   - *"Next,* we will plant the seeds in the soil."
   - *"Then,* we will water it."
   - *"Last,* we will watch our plant grow."

3. Follow-up by having children draw the procedures on the Record Sheet on page 117.

Tip! Make several sets of order-word cards to place in the writing center for students to use as a guide.

Name _____

My Record Sheet
Observe each week and draw below.

Date _____

First

Date _____

Then

Date _____

Next

Date _____

Last

Sequencing: Connecting Words

(WRITING ELEMENT–LAYOUT/FLOW

Like *first*, *then*, *next*, and *last*, connecting words help move the reader along. They guide the reader and add a certain clarity to a story. The following mini-lesson helps students use connecting words to "connect the dots" of the plot elements of their stories.

What to Do:

1. Prior to the lesson, make a list of connecting words on chart paper. (See sample chart below.) Also make copies of the connecting words on pages 120 and 121 for each student. If card stock is available and the school copy machine can use card stock, you might reproduce the pages on card stock for durability.

2. A day or so before the mini-lesson, give children the copies you made. If the cards have not been reproduced on card stock, ask children to glue the pages to oaktag or cardboard to make them sturdier. Then have children cut apart the cards. Demonstrate how to punch a hole in the upper left corner of each card with a hole punch, then bind the cards together with yarn, a brass fastener, or a binder ring. (This could also be a take-home activity.)

3. On the day of the mini-lesson, gather children to the reading center. Explain that today's writing lesson will look at special words that help connect the ideas of a story. Without these connecting words, writing can often be choppy and readers can get confused. The connecting words help us "connect the dots" of the events that happen in a story. Discuss the words on the chart, inviting children to read the words along with you. Explain that these words often appear at the beginning of a sentence.

4. Encourage children to check stories they've already written for connecting words. Model a piece of writing, either from a student sample or a piece of literature, as you search for and highlight connecting words. Then working in pairs, have students read each other's stories to find and highlight the connecting words they used, if any. Suggest that children refer to the chart and their own set of word cards.

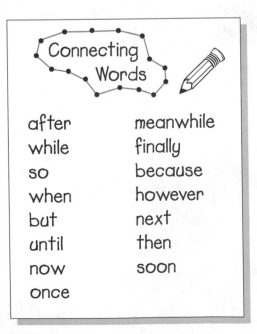

Connecting Words

after	meanwhile
while	finally
so	because
when	however
but	next
until	then
now	soon
once	

5. After a reasonable amount of time, invite children to share the connecting words they found. Let students read some of their sentences to provide examples of how the connecting words were used.

6. Culminate by asking students who found connecting words and students who did not if you could use their writing in future mini-lessons for examples to be put on transparencies.

7. Close the lesson by encouraging children to try to include connecting words in their stories.

Sample of Highlighted Writing by a Third-Grade Student

Mary and the Dog and the Wicked Witch
By Jasmine

Once long ago there lived a little girl named Mary. She had a dog named Ralph. Mary really liked Ralph.

One day Mary's dog ran into the woods. She was looking everywhere for him. Mary did not sleep all night. The next day she went on her horse to look for Ralph. She called out, "Ralph! Ralph!" She didn't hear anything. Mary got frightened! She thought he was (gulp!) hurt.

She heard little barks. That was a relief. She followed the sound and found him by a cave in a cage. She saw a wicked witch who was stirring some stew to cook Ralph in.

The witch left. Mary picked up Ralph and ran before the witch came back.

Meanwhile at the palace, the witch was finding stuff to dress up in so she could get the princess. The witch found out that the princess was not there.

Now this witch was a smart witch. She was clever too. She stayed in the palace.

When the young princess got to the palace the puppy was asleep in her arms. The witch was hiding in the princess's room. The princess was tired from walking. (Princesses need their beauty sleep.)

So when she went to sleep, the witch came out. She sprinkled some magic powder on the princess to make her sleep forever.

The next day Mary did not wake up, even when Ralph licked her on the face. Ralph got worried. Then he saw the witch. He didn't know that she was really nice. So he hid under the bed.

Now all the witch wanted was a friend and a pet. She didn't want to cook him. She wanted to eat with him. The reason she put Ralph in a cage was so he would not run away.

Then when the witch got inside she sprinkled some magic powder on the princess and said a spell that would make her wake up. She said, "Alla casam, alla cahoo, make this princess wake up," and she did.

After the princess woke up the witch was nice. The witch told her why she put her to sleep. She said, "I put you to sleep because I saw your eyes. You looked sleepy."

The nice lady lived with Mary and Ralph. And they lived happily ever after.

My Connecting Word Cards

Name: _____

when

after

but

while

until

so

now

reproducible

once	however
soon	because
then	finally
next	meanwhile

Story Building: Introducing Story Structure

(WRITING ELEMENT–LAYOUT/FLOW)

Before students can produce well-developed stories as *writers,* they need time as *readers* to analyze how stories are put together. They must become proficient at recognizing story structure in the books they read every day. When this becomes automatic, children are ready to write their own stories based on a basic story structure. The following mini-lessons introduce the idea of "story building." Students are given the opportunity to interact with story elements, first as readers, then as writers.

What to Do:

1. Prior to the lesson, select a story that is a class favorite. Any classic folktales or fairy tales work well, for the story elements are usually fairly obvious. Also create a graphic organizer on a large sheet of mural or butcher paper. Title the paper *How to Build a Story,* then draw a mountain in thick, dark marker.

2. On pages 124–127, you will find seven cards with story elements. Reproduce the cards for use with your mountain outline. If possible, reproduce the pages on card stock, then laminate them for durability.

3. Gather children to the reading center. Speculate with children why reading and writing a story might be like climbing a mountain. After children suggest ideas, explain that an author starts with a story idea, way down at the bottom of a mountain. The writer then climbs the mountain to build the story, then the writer climbs back down the mountain to reach the story's end.

4. Show children what you mean by sharing your story selection with them. Pause after each story element has been introduced. Discuss the story element with the class, and write and draw it on your story card. Place the story card on the mountain.

5. For example, the first card on the author's journey is the story **idea.** The author builds the story by adding **characters,** then a **setting.** Have students notice the graphics on each card that will assist them in remembering these important story elements.

6. Spend a long time on the **problem** element of the story, near the top of the mountain. Mention that most good stories grab us because the characters are faced with a problem.

7. Move on to explain that at the very top of the mountain, the author makes the story the most exciting. This is called the **climax.** This is the peak of the story, the part of the story that the author has been building up to.

8. Point out that the only place left to go on the mountain is down. The author needs to come up with a way to fix the problem, or find a **solution.** The bandages on the card mean "Fix It!"

9. Hold up the last card and say that all good stories come to an **end.** Point to the picture of the happy face and invite children to say, "And they all lived happily ever after!"

10. Review how the process of writing a story is like climbing a mountain—you must start at the bottom (beginning), work your way to the top (climax), then work your way back down (end).

Mountain Graphic Organizer

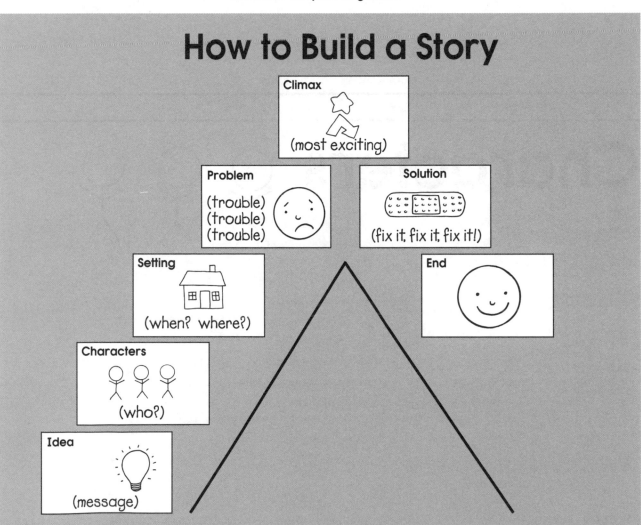

Idea

Characters

reproducible © Fearon Teacher Aids FE11021

Setting

Problem

reproducible

Climax

Solution

 © Fearon Teacher Aids FE11021

End ☺

(Cover)

reproducible

Story Building: Guided Practice

(WRITING ELEMENT–LAYOUT/FLOW)

Students have watched you "climb a mountain" as you explored the elements of a story. Now let them do the same, with a bit of guidance.

What to Do:

1. Reproduce the cards on pages 124–127 so each child has a set. Staple the cards together. Then choose a book for children to "climb." Read the story through once so that children are familiar with it.
2. Read the story again. This time, work with children to fill out their story cards to learn how the story was built. Depending on the level of your class, encourage children to draw, label, or write sentences to explain each element of the story. The cards on page 129 have been completed as examples for *The Three Little Pigs.*
3. Invite children to orally retell the story, referring to their cards for guidance. Then let children take the cards home to share the story with their families.

Tip! As a follow-up mini-lesson, remove the staples from children's cards and mix them up. Then let children work with partners to place the cards in story order. You might choose two or three student samples to laminate and place in an envelope marked *Story Sequence.* Allow students to practice putting the story together in order. You could use the sample cards on page 129 for this task as well.

Sample Story Structure

Sample Story Structure for *The Three Little Pigs*

Idea	Characters
Working Together	3 good pigs 1 bad wolf
Setting	Problem
Houses	
Climax	Solution
The Three Little Pigs	End

© Fearon Teacher Aids FE11021 reproducible 129

Idea

Working Together

Characters

bad

2

3 good pigs
1 bad wolf

good

Setting

Houses

Problem

Climax

Solution

Cover

The Three Little Pigs

End

Story Building: Independent Practice

(WRITING ELEMENT–LAYOUT/FLOW)

Now let students work in groups to explore the story elements of a favorite class book on their own.

What to Do:

1. Arrange the class into groups of four students. Present children with the book for the mini-lesson. Explain that as you read, you want them to pay special attention to the story elements that build the story.
2. Then give each group a set of story cards. Point out that there are eight cards— two for each group member. Encourage groups to discuss each story element, then decide who will be responsible for illustrating and writing about each one. One child will use the final story card to create a story cover.
3. While the groups work, circulate among them and check for accuracy, comprehension, and progress. This mini-lesson might require two sessions, depending on the level of your students. Give the groups as much time as they need.
4. Invite the groups to share their finished books with the class.

Story Building: Prewriting

(WRITING ELEMENT–LAYOUT/FLOW)

Now that you have carefully scaffolded your students' understanding of building a story, encourage them to plan stories of their own.

What to Do:

1. Gather children to the reading center, and model how to write a story using the story-structure cards (pages 124–127). Display your mountain graphic organizer from Mini-Lesson 45. Point to each story element as you discuss it aloud.

2. Buddy up students, and give each pair a set of story-structure cards. Encourage children to work together to build their stories, starting with the idea, developing characters and a setting, speculating problems and solutions, as well as the most exciting part of the story, and then describing how the story ends. (See the student sample on page 132.) Circulate among the group to offer encouragement, validation, or assistance.

3. The next day, share classmates' stories that provide good examples of building a story. Children learn best from each other!

4. As a separate mini-lesson, model how to turn these story elements into a story. Write the story for your modeling on chart paper as you refer to your own set of story-structure cards for the model. Encourage students to write their stories, referring to their story-structure cards, as well.

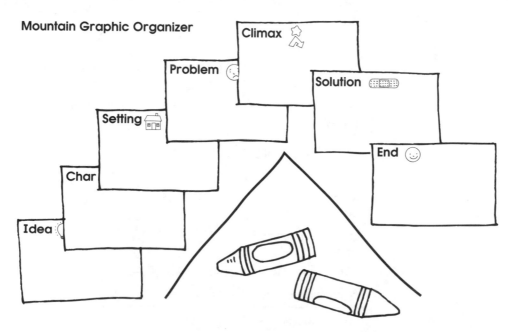

Mountain Graphic Organizer

Student Sample of Story-Structure Cards Used as a Prewriting Organizer

Idea

The zoo is sad. The sad day at the zoo.

Characters

Setting

The zoo keeper didn't take care of the zoo animals.

Problem

Now the giraffe died!!

Climax

The zoo keeper did not take care of zoo animals.

Solution

The zoo owner got some more animals and then the boss fired him. Next the zoo keeper went back to zoo school.

End

He learned how to take care of the animals. They all were happy ever after.

Story Building: Standard Story Features

(WRITING ELEMENT–LAYOUT/FLOW)

Although most stories follow the story structure explored in Mini-Lessons 45–48, various kinds of stories can include other features. The easiest way to introduce this concept is by setting up a matrix. Matrixes are graphic organizers that help students make valuable connections between concepts. The following mini-lesson explores the genre of fairy tales.

What to Do:

1. Several days before the mini-lesson, begin reading various fairy tales to the class. Read as many as possible. Analyze the stories with the class, talking about their structure.

2. Before the mini-lesson, prepare a matrix on mural or butcher paper. (See the sample on page 134.) Divide the matrix into six columns. Title the columns *Story Title, Characters (Good and Bad), Setting, Magical Element, Problem,* and *Solution/Reward.* The strips on page 135 can be used for this purpose. Also reproduce several sets of the Fairy Tale Story Cards on pages 136–138. (You will need enough for students to use in groups of four.)

3. Invite children to the reading center, and display the matrix. Explain that this big chart will show them the elements that most fairy tales have in common. Invite students to read the title and column headings with you.

4. Choose a fairy tale that children are familiar with, and model how to fill in the cards. Start with the story title. Then ask children who the "good" character is and who the "bad" character is. *What is the setting? What magical element is introduced? What is the problem the main character faces? How is the problem solved, and what is the character's reward?* As children provide ideas, fill in the cards yourself with drawings or words, and place them in the matrix.

5. Then divide the class into groups of four. Let groups choose another fairy tale to explore in this way. Make sure no fairy tales are duplicated. Instruct the groups to work cooperatively to complete each card with words or drawings, with members each being responsible for one or two. Suggest that they refer to the book, if needed, to get the correct story information.

6. As children work, circulate to offer encouragement and assistance.

7. As the cards are completed, invite the groups to the matrix to glue each card in the proper column.

8. When all the groups have finished, talk with children about the matrix. Help them conclude that all these stories—fairy tales—have some of the same story elements.

 Tip! Once students have explored the elements of fairy tales, they may be motivated to write fairy tales of their own. Encourage children to do so.

Sample Fairy Tale Matrix

Story Structure of Fairy Tales					
Story Title	Characters	Setting	Magical Element	Problem	Solution/ Reward

Story Title
Characters
Setting
Magical Element
Problem
Solution/Reward
What Makes a Fairy Tale a Fairy Tale?

Story Title

Characters

Good | Bad

reproducible

Setting

Magical Element

Problem

Solution/Reward

reproducible

Lead Sentences

(WRITING ELEMENT–LAYOUT/FLOW)

Finally, have students spruce up their stories by starting them with exciting lead sentences. When students become proficient at building story sentences and stories, they are ready to revisit their stories for this purpose. The *lead sentence* is the first sentence of the story. A good lead grabs the reader's attention and piques curiosity. By examining the first lines of your class's favorite stories, students will begin to see what you mean.

What to Do:

1. Prior to the lesson, collect class stories that have really great leading sentences. Prepare a chart titled *We Want More!* Write each lead sentence on the chart.
2. Gather the class to the reading center and explain that today's writing lesson will look at how good writers capture the attention of the reader with the very first sentence. Mention that this is called a *lead sentence*.
3. Choose a book from your selection and share with children the lead sentence. After reading the lead, close the book and exclaim, "Wow! I can't wait to find out what's going to happen next! That lead sentence really makes me want to know more!"

4. Direct children's attention to the chart, and read the corresponding lead sentence. Talk about why the lead sentence makes them want to know more. Invite a volunteer to come to the chart to circle that part of the sentence that causes the reader to be interested.
5. Continue in this way with lead sentences from other books.

Sample Chart for Lead Sentences

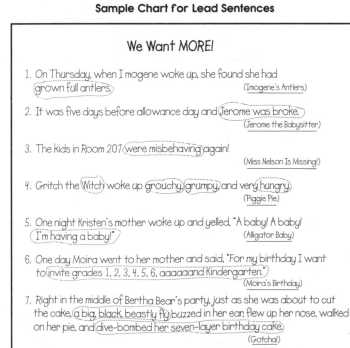

We Want MORE!

1. On Thursday, when Imogene woke up, she found she had grown full antlers. (Imogene's Antlers)

2. It was five days before allowance day and Jerome was broke. (Jerome the Babysitter)

3. The kids in Room 207 were misbehaving again! (Miss Nelson Is Missing!)

4. Gritch the Witch woke up grouchy, grumpy, and very hungry. (Piggie Pie)

5. One night Kristen's mother woke up and yelled, "A baby! A baby! I'm having a baby!" (Alligator Baby)

6. One day Moira went to her mother and said, "For my birthday I want to invite grades 1, 2, 3, 4, 5, 6, aaaaaand Kindergarten." (Moira's Birthday)

7. Right in the middle of Bertha Bear's party, just as she was about to cut the cake, a big, black, beastly fly buzzed in her ear, flew up her nose, walked on her pie, and dive-bombed her seven-layer birthday cake. (Gotcha!)

Conclusion

It is my hope that this guide has provided some ideas to help foster in young authors a love of words and composing with words, while at the same time improving their writing. As with any lesson, perhaps the biggest question is, "Will my children not only learn, but *enjoy* learning?" Yes! Children do, indeed, respond to the mini-lessons in a writer's workshop. And that's what it's all about!

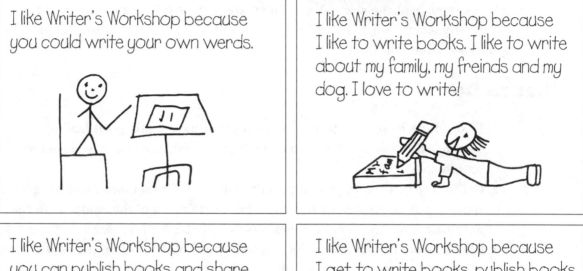

I like Writer's Workshop because you could write your own werds.

I like Writer's Workshop because I like to write books. I like to write about my family, my freinds and my dog. I love to write!

I like Writer's Workshop because you can publish books and share them with the class and everyone gets to hear.

I like Writer's Workshop because I get to write books, publish books and draw.

I like Writer's Workshop because I rily like publoshing and reading to the class. I rily like reading to the class the *most*.

Bibliography

Arnold, Tedd. *Green Wilma*. New York: Dial Books for Young Readers, 1993.

Arnold, Tedd. *Huggly Gets Dressed*. New York: Scholastic Inc., 1999.

Arnold, Tedd. *Parts*. New York: Dial Books, 1997.

Benjamin, A. H. *What If?* Wauwatosa, WI: Little Tiger Press, 1997.

Brown, Ruth. *Toad*. New York: Puffin, 1999.

Buckley, Crystal. *The Greedy Gray Octopus*. Crystal Lake, IL: Rigby Heinemann, 1988.

Carle, Eric. *Little Cloud*. New York: Putnam, 1996.

Cazet, Denys. *Never Spit on Your Shoes*. New York: Orchard Books Watts, 1993.

Christelow, Eileen. *Jerome the Babysitter*. New York: Houghton Mifflin, 1985.

Clement, Rod. *Grandpa's Teeth*. New York: HarperCollins, 1998.

Cowley, Joy. *Mrs. Wishy-Washy*. Bothell, WA: Wright Group, 1990.

Cowley, Joy. *One Stormy Night*. Bothell, WA: Wright Group, 1993.

Curtis, Jamie Lee. *Today I Feel Silly and Other Moods That Make My Day*. New York: HarperCollins, 1998.

Dalgliesh, Alice. *The Courage of Sarah Noble*. New York: Simon & Schuster Childrens, 1987.

de Paola, Tomie. *Strega Nona*. New York: Simon & Schuster, 1997.

Edwards, Pamela. *Honk!* New York: Hyperion Books for Children, 1998.

Faulkner, Keith. *The Wide-Mouthed Frog*. New York: Dial Books, 1996.

Fleming, Denise. *In the Small, Small Pond*. New York: Henry Holt & Co., 1995.

Fleming, Denise. *In the Tall, Tall Grass*. New York: Henry Holt & Co., 1995.

Flournoy, Valerie. *The Patchwork Quilt*. New York: Dial Books for Young Readers, 1985.

Fowler, Richard. *Mr. Little's Noisy Boat*. New York: Grosset and Dunlap, 1986.

Fox, Mem. *Feathers and Fools*. New York: Harcourt Brace, 1996.

Fox, Mem. *Wilfrid Gordon McDonald Partridge*. New York: Kane-Miller Book Publishers, 1985.

Godwin, Laura. *The Little White Dog*. New York: Hyperion Books, 1998.

Goss, Janet. *It Didn't Frighten Me*. Greenvale, NY: Mondo Publishing, 1995.

Graves, Kimberlee. *I Can't Sleep*. Cypress, CA: Creative Teaching Press, 1995.

Green, Robyn. *When Goldilocks Went to the House of the Bears*. Greenvale, NY: Mondo Publishing, 1995.

Gruber, Suzanne. *The Monster Under My Bed*. Mahwah, NJ: Troll Associates, 1989.

Heller, Ruth. *Kites Sail High.* New York: Putnam Publishing Group, 1988.

Heller, Ruth. *Many Luscious Lollipops.* New York: Putnam Publishing Group, 1989.

Henkes, Kevin. *Lilly's Purple Plastic Purse.* New York: Greenwillow Books, 1996.

Henkes, Kevin. *Sheila Rae, the Brave.* New York: Greenwillow Books, 1987.

Hutchins, Pat *Good-Night Owl.* New York: Simon & Schuster Childrens, 1991.

Hutchins, Pat. *Rosie's Walk.* New York: Simon & Schuster Childrens, 1998.

Jackson, Alison. *I Know an Old Lady Who Swallowed a Pie.* New York: Dutton Children's Books, 1997.

Joosse, Barbara M. *Mama, Do You Love Me?* New York: Chronicle Books, 1991.

Jorgensen, Gail. *Gotcha!* New York: Scholastic Inc., 1997.

Jorgensen, Gail. *On a Dark and Scary Night.* Crystal Lake, IL: Rigby Books, 1988.

Kroll, Steven. *Oh, Tucker.* Cambridge, MA: Candlewick Press, 1998.

London, Jonathan. *Froggy Gets Dressed.* New York: Penguin Books, 1997.

Marshall, James. *Goldilocks and the Three Bears.* New York: Scholastic Books, 1998.

Marshall, James. *Miss Nelson Is Missing!* Boston, MA: Houghton Mifflin, 1977.

Martin, Bill, Jr. *Polar Bear, Polar Bear, What Do You Hear?* New York: Henry Holt & Co., 1997.

Mayer, Mercer. *There's a Nightmare in My Closet.* New York: Dial Books, 1968.

McHennessy, John Patrick Norman. *The Boy Who Was Always Late.* New York: Dragonfly, 1999.

Munsch, Robert. *Alligator Baby.* Buffalo, NY: Firefly Books Ltd., 1997.

Munsch, Robert. *Angela's Airplane.* Buffalo, NY: Firefly Books Ltd., 1988.

Munsch, Robert. *Moria's Birthday.* Ontario, Canada: Annick Press, 1989.

Munsch, Robert. *Pigs.* Buffalo, NY: Firefly Books Ltd., 1995.

Palatini, Margie. *Piggie Pie.* New York: Houghton Mifflin, 1998.

Parkes, Brenda. *Three Little Pigs.* DesPlaines, IL: Heineman Library, 1987.

Pfister, Marcus. *The Rainbow Fish.* New York: North-South Books, 1996.

Pilkey, Dav. *Dog Breath! The Horrible Terrible Trouble with Hally Tosis.* New York: Scholastic Inc., 1994.

Plourde, Lynn. *Pigs in the Mud in the Middle of the Road.* New York: Scholastic Inc., 1997.

Polacco, Patricia. *My Rotten Redheaded Older Brother.* New York: Simon & Schuster Books for Young Readers, 1994.

Pollock, Yevonne. *The Old Man's Mitten.* Greenvale, NY: Mondo Publishing, 1994.

Raschka, Chris. *Yo! Yes?* New York: Orchard Books, 1993.

Richler, Mordecai. *Jacob Two-Two Meets the Hooded Fang.* New York: Random Books for Young Readers, 1994.

Rosen, Michael. *Avalanche.* Cambridge, MA: Candlewick Press, 1998.

Scieszka, Jon. *The True Story of the Three Little Pigs.* New York: Puffin, 1997.

Shields, Carol. *Saturday Night at the Dinosaur Stomp.* Cambridge, MA: Candlewick Press, 1997.

Small, David. *Imogene's Antlers.* New York: Crown Books for Young Readers, 1988.

Snapshot Books. *Action Pops.* New York: DK Publishing, 1995.

Spier, Peter. *Oh, Were They Ever Happy!* New York: Doubleday, 1978.

Stieg, William. *Sylvester and the Magic Pebble.* New York: Simon & Schuster Childrens, 1987.

Tolhurst, Marilyn. *Somebody and the Three Blairs.* New York: Orchard Books, 1994.

Vaughan, Marcia. *The Sandwich That Max Made.* Crystal Lake, IL: Rigby, 1989.

Vaughan, Marcia. *Snap!* New York: Scholastic Inc., 1996.

Viorst, Judith. *Alexander and the Terrible, Horrible, No Good, Very Bad Day.* New York: Simon & Schuster Childrens, 1972.

Waber, Bernard. *Ira Sleeps Over.* Boston, MA: Houghton Mifflin, 1975.

Wilder, Laura Ingalls. *Dance at Grandpa's.* New York: HarperCollins, 1995.

Williams, Linda. *The Little Old Lady Who Was Not Afraid of Anything.* New York: HarperCollins, 1988.

Williams, Rozanne Lanczak. *Five Little Monsters.* Cypress, CA: Creative Teaching Press, 1995.

Williams, Rozanne Lanczak. *Ten Monsters in a Bed.* Cypress, CA: Creative Teaching Press, 1996.

Williams, Rozanne Lanczak. *What Do You See?* Cypress, CA: Creative Teaching Press, 1994.

Williams, Rozanne Lanczak. *Where Do Monsters Live?* Cypress, CA: Creative Teaching Press, 1995.

Williams, Vera B. *A Chair for My Mother.* New York: Greenwillow Books, 1982.

Wood, Audrey. *Elbert's Bad Word.* New York: Harcourt Brace, 1996.

Wood, Audrey. *The Napping House.* Orlando, FL: Harcourt Brace, 1991.

Wood, Audrey. *The Tickle Octopus.* San Diego, CA: Harcourt Brace Janovich, 1994.

References

Atwell, Nancie. *In the Middle: New Understandings About Writing, Reading, and Learning.* 2nd ed. Portsmouth, NH: Boynton/Cook, 1998.

Atwell, Nancie. *In the Middle: Writing, Reading, and Learning with Adolescents.* Portsmouth, NH: Boynton/Cook, 1991.

Bruno, Janet. *Book Cooks.* Cypress, CA: Creative Teaching Press, 1991.

Calkins, Lucy. *The Art of Teaching Writing.* Portsmouth, NH: Heinemann, 1994.

Graves, Donald. *Build a Literate Classroom (Reading/Writing Teacher's Companion).* Portsmouth, NH: Heinemann, 1991.

Graves, Donald. *A Fresh Look at Writing.* Portsmouth, NH: Heinemann, 1994.

Kieczykowski, Carol. *Primary Writer's Workshop.* Torrance, CA: Fearon Teacher Aids, 1996.

Pinnell, Gay Su and Irene C. Fountas. *Guided Reading.* Portsmouth, NH: Heinemann, 1996.

Spandel, Vicki and Richard J. Stiggins. *Creating Writers: Linking Writing Assessment and Instruction.* Reading, MA: Addison Wesley Publishing Co., 1996.

Whisler, Nancy and Judy Williams. *Literature and Cooperative Learning: Pathways to Literacy.* Sacramento, CA: Literature Cooperative, 1990.